The Beginner's Guide to
Everyday Vegan
Cooking

The Beginner's Guide to

Everyday Vegan

Cooking

The Ultimate Starter Handbook for New Vegans

Bianca Haun & Sascha Naderer

Creators of ElephantasticVegan.com

Skyhorse Publishing

Skyhorse Publishing books may be purchased in bulk at special discounts for sales promotion, corporate gifts, fund-raising, or educational purposes. Special editions can also be created to specifications. For details, contact the Special Sales Department, Skyhorse Publishing, 307 West 36th Street, 11th Floor, New York, NY 10018 or info@skyhorsepublishing.com.

Skyhorse® and Skyhorse Publishing® are registered trademarks of Skyhorse Publishing, Inc.®, a Delaware corporation.

Visit our website at www.skyhorsepublishing.com.

10 9 8 7 6 5 4 3 2 1

Library of Congress Cataloging-in-Publication Data is available on file.

Cover design by Jane Sheppard

Cover photo by Bianca Haun and Sascha Naderer

Print ISBN: 978-1-5107-4717-3

Ebook ISBN: 978-1-5107-4720-3

Printed in China

TABLE OF CONTENTS

HI!

This Is Us

Sascha and I (Bianca) are two foodies who went vegan and fell in love with food all over again. After learning about the impact of animal agriculture on the planet, the wrenchingly cruel practices in slaughterhouses, and the positive health effects a plant-based diet can have on the body, we began a vegan way of life in 2012. *The Beginner's Guide to Everyday Vegan Cooking* is our way of helping other vegan beginners adjust to their new lifestyle.

Born and raised in Austria, a meat-focused country like so many, I want to prove that a vegan diet is not only possible, but also delicious, for everyone. After following a vegan lifestyle for two years, I started the blog *Elephantastic Vegan* to share my favorite plant-based recipes. Over the last two years of food blogging, I've shared over 300 plant-based recipes, a handful of vegan travel reports, kitchen hacks, product reviews, and guides for vegans, the latter being published in a blog section dedicated for new vegans. Thus, the inspiration for *The Beginner's Guide to Everyday Vegan Cooking* was born.

Sascha is a lover of food that cooks itself, so all kinds of soups, stews, goulashes, and curries are usually his area of expertise. While he does not enjoy baking, he certainly loves eating all kinds of baked goods, especially anything bread-related. While I'm in the kitchen whipping up snacks, he prepares the drinks to make sure no one is thirsty. Showing people how delicious plant-based food can be is our favorite way of sparking people's interest in a vegan lifestyle.

AN INTRODUCTION

Why We Went Vegan
and Why We Didn't Do It Sooner

It all started when Bianca and I were on holiday in the United States. We had stuffed our faces with so much meat and eggs that we got sick of it, so Bianca suggested we try a popular vegan food chain in Philadelphia where we had our first vegan burger. This. This felt great. And not just great, it felt right.

On that same trip, Bianca bought a copy of *Eating Animals* by Jonathan Foer. In this book, the author writes about the implications of buying and eating meat, from suffering animals to damaged environments and what it does to our bodies. Soon after, we watched the *Earthlings* documentary together. We're not going to lie. It's an intense documentary with real scenes from slaughterhouses, pet stores, and puppy mills. It shows how animals are exploited by humans in five ways: pets, food, clothing, entertainment, and science. It was the hardest documentary we've ever watched, but it was so worth it. That same night, we swore off animal products. We had been on-and-off vegetarians before, so we were already having conversations about the ethics of food before we decided to switch. Our first vegan experience was not some kind of big revelation, but it still impacted us like only a few decisions ever would. We decided to give veganism a try.

Of course, changes like these are hard. Especially when you have been eating a certain way your whole life. So, our change was gradual. At first, we would have a good number of vegan and vegetarian meals per week with the rare portion of fish here and there. Then, we started to swap out foods from our previous lifestyle with vegan alternatives; veggie sausages, veggie bacon, and veggie cheese played a huge part in our daily diets. It was a great way for us to let go of the animal products without actually having to rip the Band-Aid off completely. We still indulge in those substitutes sometimes, but nowhere near as often. After that, we decided to eat vegan at home and only have the vegetarian options at restaurants, or with friends and relatives.

When we eventually went 100 percent vegan, restaurants had started to offer vegan options, supermarkets offered a solid lineup of vegan products, and the people closest to us had a decent understanding of our ethical standpoint. During that time, we learned that food is an emotional topic for everybody, and it's very important to respect other people's life choices, even if you sometimes find yourself being unrightfully challenged. This is why we choose to refer our choice as a *don't* rather than a *can't*. "I don't eat cheese" is a statement, while "I can't have cheese" is a restriction; something debatable.

"Come on, a little sausage can't hurt, right?"

"Thanks, I don't eat meat," is always clearer than "Sorry, I can't have this sausage." Of course you can. You just choose not to.

People will offer you numerous what-about-isms and sometimes they'll try to flat-out prove you wrong. Just remember that this is all part of the learning process. Also, get comfortable with the fact that people have different views on veganism. There are always things that will lead you to think "Maybe I'm not a vegan after all." And maybe those things are sometimes even right. So please don't do it for the label. Be as good as you can be, or as Gandhi said: "Be the change you wish to see in the world."

Veganism is not a label. It's not a challenge. a streak, a club, or an elite. It's a decision, and it's been one of our best.

Part I

BEGINNERS' TIPS YOU WILL FIND IN THIS BOOK

Bianca's Kitchen Hacks

Vegans are a diverse group of people, but whether you're a rookie cook or an advanced artist in the kitchen, knowing your way around vegan recipes is never a bad thing. That's why I've compiled a list of little tricks and shortcuts and sprinkled them throughout the recipes for the savvy vegan cook. We like to call these *Bianca's Kitchen Hacks*.

Sascha's Landmine Situations

Have you ever been in a social situation where you run into the danger of reverting back into old habits? Believe me, I've been there more than once, and people make it easy to fall back on your promises: A coworker can't finish their cheesy pizza and is about to toss it. Grandma tried, but ended up using butter in your birthday cake. You're drunk and you think that this kebab sandwich will save your life. We call those events *landmine situations*—things we'd love to avoid but sometimes have a hard time avoiding.

BASIC EQUIPMENT AND INGREDIENTS

You don't need lots of fancy equipment to cook vegan food. For many recipes, a cutting board, knife, and pot will do, but if you want to invest in cooking equipment, a high-powered blender for creamy soups and sauces or a food processor for "nice" cream and quickly chopping veggies may be worth looking into. We have raided our pantry, fridge, and freezer and written down our pantry essentials for you. If you have these basic ingredients on hand, you will be able to make most of the recipes in this book.

Kitchen Tools

Being vegan isn't that difficult and you won't need many big items to create your favorite dish. However, sometimes a little help is a great way to get cooking. So, besides the usual things that make a good kitchen great, we wouldn't want to miss these three things in our lives.

A high-powered blender makes it easy to make creamy sauces, soups, smoothies, and shakes.

A food processor is a great addition for any kitchen. You can chop up veggies, make a base for falafel or pesto really quick.

Nut milk bags or fine cheesecloths are a great investment if you're making nut milks at home regularly.

Pantry Essentials

Pantry essentials that you should always have at home include garlic, onions, ginger, lemons, bananas, and cocoa powder. However, there are many more things that will make it easier for you to create a vegan dish from scratch. Here's a list of items that we think should be a part of every vegan's pantry.

Grains and pasta are things you should always have at home for spontaneous cravings and to make quick veggie bowls. We like quinoa, couscous, white and brown rice, and different kinds of pasta such as penne, spaghetti, and lasagna sheets.

Oils such as coconut oil for baking, olive oil for pesto and breads, and canola oil for frying at home are usually on hand at our house.

Canned legumes such as chickpeas, lentils, and black beans are a great base for stews and curries. We also use canned chickpeas for hummus and falafel. Of course, you can soak and cook dried legumes instead.

Nuts and seeds are a great source of protein, fats, and fiber. We use cashews, walnuts, almonds, chia seeds, flaxseeds, poppy seeds, sesame seeds, and sunflower seeds in our recipes.

White sugar is not necessarily vegan since bone char is often used to decolorize the sugar. Make sure the white sugar you buy is organic, because these are not filtered through bone char. You can always research if your favorite sugar brand is vegan. Beet sugar and coconut sugar should be a safe bet, too.

Tomato passata is great when you are in need of a quick pasta sauce, but it also does well in stews, curries, or soups. You could also use canned crushed tomatoes in most of our recipes.

Spices and herbs such as salt, curry powder, paprika powder, onion powder, and garlic powder are basics. To make tofu taste like eggs, we use kala namak, which is a Himalayan black salt with a high sulfur content that gives tofu scramble its typical smell and taste. As for herbs, dried or fresh oregano, rosemary, basil, dill, and thyme are good to have at home. These will make any meal better.

Nut butters are a great source of protein and fiber. We love using almond butter to make our caramel sauce, and peanut butter for sauces and our African-inspired peanut butter stew.

All-purpose flour is a great starter for everything bread-related. You should keep it at home at all times. If you want to use whole wheat flour or spelt flour in the recipes, oftentimes a mix of all-purpose flour and whole grain flours makes the best, workable doughs.

Activated dried yeast is the rising agent for yeasty doughs such as pizza and cinnamon rolls.

Other great foods for vegans with a sweet tooth to have available include dried fruits such as dates, raisins, and cranberries, oats, and liquid sweeteners such as maple/brown rice/agave syrup.

On the savory side, nori is an edible seaweed and the perfect way to give your dish that fishy flavor you maybe sometimes crave. Plus, you can also use nori to make maki sushi.

Nutritional yeast is the secret ingredient in vegan cooking to make things taste cheesy. It is deactivated yeast that can be bought in flakes or as a powder. Don't confuse this with baker's yeast or brewing yeast.

Tahini is a paste made from ground sesame seeds. It's quite bitter on its own but delicious in dressing and dips when balanced out with maple syrup.

Liquid smoke is a very potent liquid that adds a smoky flavor to all kinds of protein such as tofu or tempeh.

Vital wheat gluten is a hydrated form of gluten that can be found in wheat flour. It is used when making seitan. Note: if you've got a gluten intolerance, this one isn't for you.

Fridge and Freezer Staples

Of all the vegans we know, there are certain foods most of them always have in their fridge.

Tofu is rich in protein. Silky tofu is great for desserts, while firm tofu is best for tofu scramble and stir-fries. Smoked tofu adds a lovely new flavor component to a dish.

Plant-based milk such as rice milk is our favorite for baking and cooking, while almond milk is our favorite for cereal. Oat milk, hemp milk and many nut-based milks are great, too! Make sure you use unsweetened plant-based milk when you use it in savory dishes. Try out different types of plant-based milks and brands, you'll definitely find one you'll like!

Miso paste is a traditional Japanese paste made out of fermented soybeans. It's very salty and sweet and great to add flavor to soups.

Vegan puff pastry might not be available everywhere, but it's worth keeping an eye out for it because it's a pain to make from scratch. Pepperidge Farm's puff pastry dough is vegan but it is always a good idea to check the ingredients before buying in case they change the recipe.

Try to always have frozen peas, spinach, and bananas at your disposal. While peas and spinach are a great addition to almost every dish, frozen bananas make a great treat if they're being put in a blender, dipped in hot chocolate, or used as an alternative for eggs when baking a cake.

HOW TO COOK GRAINS

Here's a simple overview of the ratios and instructions we follow to cook the grains used in this cookbook.

White Rice

Ratio: 1 cup rice to 1½ cups water

Add 1½ cups water, 1 cup rice, and a dash of salt in a pot. Put the lid on and cook it on medium heat. Let it simmer for about 10 to 15 minutes until the rice has completely absorbed the water.

Brown Rice

Ratio: 1 cup rice to 2 cups water

Add 2 cups water, 1 cup rice, and a dash of salt in a pot. Put the lid on and cook on medium heat. Let it simmer for about 25 to 30 minutes until the rice has completely absorbed the water.

Couscous

Ratio: 1 cup couscous to 1½ cups water

In a large pot, bring the water to a boil. Take the pot off the hot plate, add in the couscous, and put the lid on. Let it sit for a few minutes until the couscous has completely absorbed all the water. Then fluff the couscous with a large wooden spoon. Pro Tip: Add any spices you want into the boiling water. That way, the couscous will absorb the spices, too.

Quinoa

Ratio: 1 cup quinoa to 2 cups water

Rinse the quinoa. Then, add quinoa and water to a pot and cook it on medium heat with the lid on. Let it simmer for about 20 minutes until the quinoa has completely absorbed all the water.

SUBSTITUTES THAT WILL MAKE YOU (ALMOST) FORGET ABOUT NON-VEGAN FOOD

We know that many non-vegan food items are delicious. As a matter of fact, a great number of people don't go vegan because they dislike the taste of chicken fingers, late-night kebabs, and grilled cheese, but for ethical reasons. This is why non-vegan cravings are a common and completely normal thing. But don't worry, there are many foods that will help you fight the urge to order cheese pizza, buy a meatball sub, or get yourself a treat of buttered popcorn.

Meat: If you're looking to substitute meat, there are many great choices, the obvious and most well-known option being tofu. However, you should give other meat substitutes, such as tempeh or seitan a try. For maximum protein, check out textured vegetable protein, which comes in different shapes and sizes and can be used to substitute (almost) every meat product.

Fish: This is a tricky one. Alternative products never seem to get fish right. But that's okay. We recommend mixing tofu with nori (a seaweed) to fight sudden seafood cravings.

Eggs for baking: Many people think that eggs are indispensable for baking a cake. They're not. Add more baking powder, mashed bananas, or apple purée. Chia eggs or flax eggs are a great way to substitute eggs in both sweet and savory baked goods. Mix one tablespoon of ground chia or ground flaxseeds with three tablespoons water and let it sit for about 5 minutes until goopy, then you can use it just like you would an egg.

Milk: Easy. Plant-based drinks made from hemp, almond, cashew, hazelnut, coconut, rice, oat, or even pistachios and macadamia nuts have been around for a while. Try to experiment what you like most; it's a fun tasting experience!

Butter: There are many varieties of vegan butter available in stores. Beware of margarine, which can contain animal products such as whey or lactose. Coconut oil is also great.

Cream: For heavy cream, try unsweetened coconut milk. For whipped cream, definitely check out whipped coconut cream. If you're not into coconut, many stores offer a good variety of alternative products based on oats and rice.

Gelatin: Use agar-agar flakes. It's easy and not even half as tricky as gelatin can be.

Cheese: Boy, there's a whole book to be written about vegan cheese, but we'll keep it short. For Parmesan, try our Cashew Parmesan (see on pg. 17) or neat vegan cheese sauce (see on pg. 18). There are also many people who try to create vegan cheeses on the internet, so if you need inspiration for an advanced endeavor like this, make sure to check out vegan cheese makers online.

HOW TO AVOID ARGUING WITH SKEPTICS

Dietary preferences are not just an issue for vegans or vegetarians. A huge portion of the world's population has one reason or another for not eating certain foods, either for ethical or religious reasons, intolerances, or simply not liking something.

If you are someone who eats "outside the norm," chances are that you have been confronted with some provoking one-liners or even ignorant mistruths about your choices by colleagues, friends, or family members. And if that happens, it's not always easy to let it slide. Food is an emotional topic. Everybody's an expert, everybody has an opinion, and everybody firmly believes that what they're doing is the right thing. So do you, and so do they.

Even in countries where the mere need for food has become a non-issue, food itself still plays a very important role to the majority of people. Whether we talk about where, what, when, and how much to eat, how to prepare food, and who to share our meals with, choosing to eat or not eat a certain thing or prepare it in a special way can lead to a variety of social repercussions ranging from friendly banter to a full-blown argument and subsequently social seclusion. Party over.

However, sometimes you just don't want to find yourself in a situation where you dispute over what you are (or aren't) eating, when all you want to do is enjoy the company of your family and friends. So, if you're prone to disputes over your dietary preference, here's a list of pointers that will help you avoid being the center of attention just because of what you do or do not eat.

Try to See Where They're Coming From

Chances are you haven't been vegan or vegetarian for the span of your whole life. Maybe you've been an avid meat-eater for many years. Sometimes it's hard to understand the other person's position, especially when your dietary preference has become the norm for you. But remember, food is an emotional topic, so people don't appreciate being told that they are responsible for the death and torturing of living, breathing beings.

They may do things that you find ethically questionable, but that doesn't mean they're evil. Some of them will take some lighthearted jabs at you, but a lot of it comes out of insecurity and curiosity. Be able to take a joke—even if you've heard it for the millionth time. And you will hear many jokes—millions of times. For a lot of people, this is a playful way to explore. Our advice? Let them! Be in on it.

Invite Them to Dinner

When you see that another person's remarks about your preference come out of ignorance or lack of education, lecturing them is the worst way to stay out of trouble. We all know what they say about know-it-alls, so instead of telling them about veganism, show them. Invite them. Feed them a home-cooked meal or treat them to a quick lunch at your favorite falafel place. Give the other person a chance to have a taste of your everyday life. It's a friendly way to defuse a situation that could easily ruin your socializing experience.

Tell a Little White Lie

It's not a good thing to lie. It's also not a good thing to betray the things you believe in. However, we all have those days where we really, really want to avoid discussing our dietary preferences. So, if the setting allows it, another option is to not talk about it or maybe even lie if the topic comes up. Sometimes you're not in the mood for taking jokes. Sometimes you don't want to invite your grumpy colleague for hummus. So, if the person you are talking to isn't really that close to you, it's no big deal to tell a lie or say nothing. Maybe you are lactose intolerant, maybe you're still full from that big lunch you've had. Anything that gets you out of the situation. We wouldn't recommend doing it for long, though.

Ask Them to Talk Later

You know the situation: it's a buzzing party, the music is loud, there are drinks involved, and you thoroughly enjoy the company of your friends and family members. And then someone catches you reading the packaging of the potato chips, looking to see if they are vegan and ready to stuff your salt-craving face with. And you want nothing to do with debating your dietary preferences right now.

In this situation, try to leave the topic be, at least for now. Nobody wants to lose a debate in front of an audience. If you think that the other person really is curious about veganism, offer to talk about big topics like this another time if they're interested. Of course, if you're not a fan of small talk and enjoy lengthy, drunken conversations, go ahead!

Agree to Disagree

If the other person is obviously not interested in your point and just wants to talk, but not listen, let them. You don't need to please everyone with your lifestyle. Neither do they. People have different ethical standpoints when it comes to food, and while it can be hard to accept that, sometimes the right thing to do is just walk away and move on.

HOW TO RESPOND TO SKEPTICS

As someone with a dietary preference, you will often find people who are curious, which leads to a wide range of reactions, starting from childlike curiosity to complete negation. Somewhere in between are the people who are willing to listen and learn, but they still have their own way of doing things; you might not see eye to eye when it comes to your individual preferences, and that's okay.

People often want to know more about veganism, but are skeptical. And they should be. Changing your lifestyle like that is a huge change. It's emotional, it's personal and it's messy. The skeptics in your life will repeat themselves and at times you may think that people will do anything just to annoy you with age-old questions and long-debunked myths. It's not that. Just like you, they are on a journey somewhere, and these questions matter to them. So, try to give them some answers, even if you feel like an old cassette tape. To make things easier, we've provided you with our guidelines on how to respond to skeptics.

"Are you really a vegan if you buy vegan cheese and meat alternatives?"

You've heard it all before, at work, from relatives or friends. "Why'd you go for cheese alternatives if you're a vegan?" "Shouldn't you be sticking to veggies and stuff?" Well, as you may know, the answers are not always that easy.

First of all, to many people, going vegan is an ethical choice that has nothing to do with the taste of crispy bacon, goat cheese, or honey over frozen yogurt. Veganism is, first and foremost, about negating the use of animal products in your life. Sure, there are many things that go along with it—many vegans also buy fair-trade coffee, live a healthy lifestyle, and yes, many of us like to talk about it.

Savvy companies have come up with clever alternative products that are free of meat, milk, and eggs. These products often resemble tastes and textures of the non-vegan foods many of us grew up with, but also come with the same downsides as their non-vegan counterparts; rich in sodium, sugar, and fats, those vegan nuggets can come close to the real thing in more ways than one. For some people, this makes the transition easier. And that's okay, because the level of enjoyment is not a factor in ethical decisions. Vegan alternatives can sometimes be a trade-off: Can you accept 60 percent of the original taste for good conscience? Your call.

"We are carnivores, we're at the top of the food chain. We need protein to survive. It's only natural."

This is a point often made by hardcore carnivores and brings a lot of emotional baggage to the table. In many western societies, food has transitioned from a basic necessity for survival to a more sophisticated issue that is influenced by cultural background, individual dietary preferences, and/or restrictions. In other words, food is an emotional topic and since every person on earth has to eat, they might as well have an opinion about it.

The points to be made in that kind of discussion are almost too many to list. Carnivore? The human is an omnivore and can survive many kinds of diets—neither eating meat nor veganism are the only answer. Protein? Tempeh, tofu, and soy protein contain lots of protein. Not natural? Also, while we can consume meat, we're the only known species that has to cook it first.

"You can't change the world all by yourself, can you?"

Not only vegans get this question. Anyone who wants to be part of a global change finds themselves confronted with it. The answer is simple: Of course not. This book is not going to solve everything, you are not going to make veganism the norm, and veganism won't end world hunger. Not immediately.

So why bother doing something, even though your personal impact is just a small one? Throwing in famous quotes to end an argument is easy, but I'll do it anyway. Ever heard of that super-famous Gandhi quote, "Be the change you want to see in the world?" That's why.

For most people, making the switch to veganism, working out, or getting creative can often be a gradual change without immediate results. And yet, many people keep at it. Eventually, intrinsic motivation leads to progress.

Baby steps. Make sure to take them.

"I get that you avoid meat, but milk and eggs?"

Milk and eggs don't kill animals, so they're good to go, right? Well, not exactly. While it's true that animals don't get killed directly to acquire milk and eggs, the industrial production is still often linked to suffering and death. For example, since male chickens can't lay eggs, they are not seen as efficient or useful and the baby birds are often gassed or shredded. No, it's probably not different in your country. Another widespread myth is that cows love to be milked. In order to give milk, a dairy cow has to be impregnated all the time, which is exhausting, painful, and leads to an earlier death. Many films such as *Cowspiracy* and *Forks over Knives* and literature such as *Eating Animals* by Jonathan Safran Foer or *The Omnivore's Dilemma* by Michael Pollan have covered this, so if you didn't know about it, you've got tons of material to watch, read, and discuss!

"I could never go through with this."

You don't have to ask anybody to go vegan for this statement to come up. For many people, this is a conversation ender, so you might just want to leave it at that. However, if you're getting a vibe that they want you to weigh in, there is of course always one question to ask: "Can you do one vegan meal per week? How about two?"

This is important, because almost nobody goes vegan in an instant. To most people, it's a process, and intrinsic motivation combined with a basic knowledge about how to cook are the best helpers you can have. While intrinsic motivation gives you the edge to go the extra mile when reading lists of ingredients in the grocery store, knowing how to cook will let you stay away from guilty pleasures.

Nobody has to go vegan cold tofurkey. Take your time to adjust. Create habits that stick.

BASICS

CASHEW PARMESAN

This Cashew Parmesan is an all-time staple in our household. We sprinkle it over all our pasta dishes, risottos, or pizza. It really works with everything and anything! Our Cashew Parmesan recipe takes only a couple of minutes to make and it stores for weeks and weeks. (If you haven't devoured all of it before then, that is.)

Makes: *1 cup* | Time: *5 min*

Instructions

1. Put all ingredients in a kitchen processor and pulse until a fine powder is created that resembles Parmesan.

2. Sprinkle over all kinds of pasta dishes, pizza, or risotto.

3. Store the vegan Parmesan in an airtight glass jar at room temperature for 1 to 2 months without problems.

Ingredients

1 cup (130g) raw cashews*

2 tablespoons nutritional yeast flakes

¾ teaspoon salt

*You could also use blanched almonds or substitute with sunflower seeds for a nut-free alternative.

BASIC VEGAN CHEESE SAUCE

This vegan cheese sauce is perfect for various purposes. It's delicious on lasagna, pasta bakes, pizza, in mac & cheese, or to eat as a dip. It's ooey-gooey and everything you've ever wanted in a vegan cheese sauce!

Makes: ¾ *cup* | Time: *5 min*

Ingredients

- 2 tablespoons coconut oil
- ⅓ cup (40 g) all-purpose flour
- ½ teaspoon salt
- ¼ teaspoon paprika powder
- ¼ teaspoon curry powder
- ⅓ cup (20 g) nutritional yeast
- ½ cup (120 ml) water

Instructions

1. Heat the coconut oil in a small pot on low heat.

2. Once the oil is a complete liquid, add in the flour and whisk.

3. Add the salt, paprika powder, and curry powder and whisk again.

4. Then, add the nutritional yeast and whisk again. It should be clumpy—that's normal, don't worry.

5. Add the water and whisk on the lowest heat setting for about 1 minute until the sauce thickens nicely. If it gets too thick (or if you want to reheat at a later time) you can add a little bit more water and whisk again and it should be good as new.

6. Use it as a dip, pour it over some lasagna or pizza or whatever you like, and enjoy!

HOMEMADE SEITAN

Seitan is made by rinsing the starch from wheat flour over and over again, which is quite time-consuming. Thankfully, there's a lifesaver called vital wheat gluten, which allows us to make seitan much, much quicker. Seitan does not have any real taste itself. Just like tofu, you can consider it a blank canvas for you to paint on, so make sure to add lots of spices to give it a delicious taste!

Makes: *1 log* | Time: *1 hour*

Instructions

1. Combine the dry ingredients in a large mixing bowl. In a separate bowl combine the wet ingredients and whisk. Add the combined wet ingredients to the dry ingredients and mix everything with a large spoon, then use your hands to knead the mixture for a couple of minutes until it's stretchy and all of the ingredients are incorporated. Shape into a loaf.

2. Cover the seitan loaf in plastic wrap or cheesecloth and knot the edges.

3. Bring enough water in a large pot to a boil, then reduce the heat and simmer the seitan for about 45 minutes.

4. Remove the plastic wrap or cheesecloth, cut the seitan in slices, chunks, or whatever you need for the recipe you want to make. I like to pan-fry the seitan quickly so the sides get crispy before using it in the recipe.

5. Keep the seitan in an airtight container in the fridge for up to 3 days.

Ingredients

1 cup (130 g) vital wheat gluten

¼ cup (15 g) nutritional yeast

¼ cup (30 g) all-purpose flour

½ teaspoon salt

1 teaspoon garlic powder

1 teaspoon onion powder

1 teaspoon dried basil

1 teaspoon dried thyme

1 teaspoon smoked paprika

½ cup (120 ml) water

1 tablespoon soy sauce

2 tablespoons tomato paste

1 teaspoon olive oil

DATE-SWEETENED ALMOND MILK

Plant-based milks are staples in a vegan diet, and the good news is that it's actually not hard to make them yourself. This is a basic recipe for naturally sweetened almond milk, but you can easily remove the dates for an unsweetened version. You can also add maple syrup, chocolate, or ground vanilla to give it an even sweeter twist. Note: A quality nut milk bag, preferably nylon, is even more important than a high-speed blender. This really makes a difference and makes your nut milk super silky and soft!

Makes: *4 cups* | Time: *10 min + soaking time overnight*

Ingredients

- 1 cup (150 g) blanched almonds (or regular ones, but the milk will be a bit darker)
- 12 dates
- 4 cups (1 liter) water (use less if you want to make it thicker)
- 1 pinch of salt

Instructions

1. Soak the almonds overnight. Drain and rinse the almonds.

2. Put the almonds, dates, water, and salt in a high-speed blender and blend on high for 1 to 2 minutes. At this point, you can add additional flavors like cocoa powder* or ground vanilla if you want!

3. Cover a strainer with a nut milk bag for the smoothest results, and place it in a bowl. Alternatively, you can use a cheesecloth or breathable clean kitchen towel. Then, pour the almond milk in the nut milk bag and press out excess liquid.

4. Store the milk in an airtight container and keep it in the fridge for up to 3 days.

Bianca's Kitchen Hack
How to Make Any Plant-Based Milk

You can make more than just nut milk at home. Just like you would with the nuts, you could also soak rice, oats, pumpkin seeds, hemp seeds, coconut flesh, flaxseeds, and sunflower seeds for more plant-based milk varieties. Let them soak for a few hours, blend them with water, and strain. Done.

*For a chocolate milk version, add 2 tablespoons cocoa powder per 2 cups milk.

THREE-INGREDIENT WHISK-ONLY CARAMEL SAUCE

We know, we know. This is not actually caramel sauce. While traditional caramel sauce is made out of caramelized sugar, we tried a healthier approach and found this recipe to be just as delicious as the real thing. You'll only need three ingredients for this one. Plus, you don't need to heat it up!

Makes: ¼ cup | Time: *2 min*

Instructions

1. With a small whisk, mix the almond butter, syrup, and water until smooth.

2. Let it sit for a few minutes to thicken up.

3. Serve over some nice cream (see on pg. 182) or use it in the caramel cups (see on pg. 169).

Ingredients

2 tablespoons almond butter

1 tablespoon maple syrup, rice syrup, or agave syrup

1 teaspoon water*

---

*Depending on the almond butter you're using, you might have to add a bit less or more water to reach a perfect ooey-gooey consistency.

SMALL-BATCH STRAWBERRY CHIA JAM

In our household, we don't really eat tons of jam, so when we do, we usually prepare quick little batches. This batch of strawberry chia jam can be made with just a few minutes of work. It's the perfect jam for PB&J sandwiches or to spread it on our homemade English muffins (see on pg. 113).

Makes: *¼ cup* | Time:*10 min*

Ingredients

- 1 cup (130 g) frozen strawberries
- 1 teaspoon maple syrup
- 1 teaspoon chia seeds

Instructions

1. Put the frozen strawberries in a small pot, add the maple syrup, and let them cook on medium heat until soft.

2. Mash them with a fork, add the chia seeds, and give it a quick mix.

3. Take the pot off the stove and let it sit for about an hour to thicken. After that you can use it immediately or fill a small jar and store it in the fridge for about a week.

BREAKFAST

EGGY TOFU SCRAMBLE

Tofu scramble is *the* perfect, protein-packed vegan alternative for scrambled eggs. Kala namak or Himalayan black salt is the key ingredient in this recipe and will make it taste and smell super eggy. Don't forget to play around with different add-ins, such as dried tomatoes and olives, for a Mediterranean version.

Makes: *1–2 servings* | Time: *10 min*

Instructions

1. Heat the canola oil in a large pan and scramble the tofu with your hands or use a fork to do it before adding it to the pan.

2. Add the curry powder, turmeric, and kala namak. Mix well, so the tofu turns evenly yellow.

3. Keep it on medium high heat while stirring for about 5 minutes. At this point, you can add more kala namak or other spices or herbs of choice to taste and preference. After that, it's ready to serve.

Ingredients

1 teaspoon canola oil

8 oz. (250 g) firm tofu

½ teaspoon curry powder

½ teaspoon turmeric powder

¾ teaspoon kala namak or Himalayan black salt

SWEET BANANA BREAD

What to do with bananas that are not only ripe, but *very* ripe? Usually, I'd say banana ice cream, but this banana bread will make a really delicious alternative to use up all those left-over bananas. The bread is perfectly sweet and makes a delicious breakfast, dessert, or snack.

Makes: *1 loaf* | Time: *15 min + 1½ hours baking time*

Ingredients

- 4 *very* ripe bananas
- ½ cup (120 ml) plant-based milk e.g. rice milk
- 1 tablespoon coconut oil, liquid
- ¼ cup (80 g) maple syrup + more for drizzling on top
- 1½ cups (180 g) all-purpose flour
- 1 teaspoon baking powder
- ½ teaspoon baking soda
- 1 teaspoon cinnamon powder
- ½ cup (60 g) almond meal
- 1 pinch of salt

Instructions

1. Preheat the oven to 320°F/160°C and line a loaf pan with parchment paper.

2. Peel the bananas, cut one of them in half lengthwise, and set aside. Mash the other three bananas in a bowl and add the plant-based milk, coconut oil, and maple syrup. Give it a quick mix.

3. In another large bowl, combine the flour, baking powder, baking soda, cinnamon powder, almond meal, and a pinch of salt. Whisk. Then, pour in the wet ingredients from the other bowl. Whisk it all together until combined.

4. Pour the batter in the loaf pan and add the halved banana on top.

5. Bake it in the oven for about 1½ hours or until golden brown on top. You can use a toothpick to test if your banana bread is done in the middle (see Bianca's Kitchen Hack on pg. 32).

6. Before serving, drizzle maple syrup on top and enjoy!

FLUFFY BLUEBERRY PANCAKES

Every breakfast-loving vegan should have a favorite, well-tested pancake recipe, and this is ours! We are both huge fans of blueberries, so putting them together with delicious, fluffy pancakes is almost a no-brainer. If you want, you can sub the blueberries with other fruits or use chocolate chips instead if you're feeling naughty.

Makes: *8 pancakes* | Time: *25 min*

Instructions

1. In a mixing bowl, add the flour, baking powder, and salt and give it a quick whisk. Add in the maple syrup, vanilla extract, plant-based milk, and canola oil. Whisk until incorporated.

2. Spray a flat pan or griddle with oil on medium to low heat. Add a ladle of pancake batter and add a handful of blueberries on top. Let it cook for about 1 to 2 minutes until the middle becomes bubbly and the corners set, then flip with a spatula. Let it cook on the other side for another minute until golden brown.

3. Stack the pancakes, generously garnish with the rest of the blueberries, and drizzle with maple syrup.

Ingredients

1 cup (120 g) all-purpose flour

1½ teaspoons baking powder

1 pinch of salt

2 tablespoons maple syrup + more for drizzling on top

¼ teaspoon vanilla extract

¾ cup (180 ml) unsweetened plant-based milk

1 teaspoon canola oil + more for spraying the pan with oil

1 cup (100 g) fresh blueberries

CINNAMON RAISIN FLATBREAD

This is a sweet variation of a very simple and delicious flatbread recipe. We've added cinnamon powder into the dough and topped it with raisins, which makes it an absolutely perfect breakfast for the sweet tooth on the go.

Makes: *2 flatbreads* | Time: *15 min*

Ingredients

- 1 ⅓ cups (160 g) all-purpose flour
- ½ teaspoon baking powder
- 1 teaspoon cinnamon powder
- 1 pinch of salt
- 1 teaspoon maple syrup
- ½ cup (120 ml) plant-based milk e.g. rice milk
- ¼ cup (45 g) raisins
- ½ teaspoon coconut oil for the pan

Instructions

1. Combine the flour, baking powder, cinnamon powder, and salt in a large mixing bowl. Give it a quick whisk. Add in the maple syrup and plant-based milk. Combine with a large spoon and knead with your hands until a soft dough forms. You may have to add more flour (if it's too sticky) or more plant-based milk (if it's too crumbly).

2. Divide the dough into two equal parts and roll it out until about 1-inch thick, then pour the raisins onto the dough and roll it again, so that the raisins stick to the dough. The flatbread should be about ½-inch thick now.

3. Prepare a hot pan with coconut oil and let the flatbread fry on each side for about 1 minute until brownish and bubbly.

4. Eat while it's warm and enjoy!

APPLE PIE OVERNIGHT OATS

Together with chia puddings, overnight oats are one of our favorite quick, make-ahead, no-fuss breakfast recipes. If you tend to oversleep and usually have no time for preparing breakfast in the mornings, this is the perfect food to prepare in the evenings, seal up, and take to work the next day. Easy, quick, and delicious. This version tastes like apple pie!

Makes: *1 serving* | Time: *10 min + overnight*

Instructions

1. Add the rolled oats, ½ cup of plant-based milk, ½ teaspoon of cinnamon, and ½ teaspoon of maple syrup in a glass jar and give it a good mix. Keep it in the fridge overnight.

2. The next day, peel an apple and remove the core. Cut the apple in chunks and put it in a bowl. Add ¼ teaspoon of cinnamon and give it a quick mix until the apple is evenly coated.

3. Add 2 teaspoons of plant-based milk to the overnight oats and stir to combine. Place the apple topping on top of the overnight oats, drizzle with more maple syrup, and enjoy!

Ingredients

- ½ cup (50 g) rolled oats
- ½ cup (120 ml) plant-based milk e.g. unsweetened rice milk + 2 teaspoons plant-based milk to be added the next day
- ½ teaspoon cinnamon + ¼ teaspoon cinnamon for the apple topping
- ½ teaspoon maple syrup + more for drizzling on top
- 1 small apple

HEALTHY BREAKFAST MUFFINS

These healthy muffins are 100 percent fruit-sweetened with dates, raisins, and bananas, making them the perfect breakfast muffins. They don't contain any regular flour, but oat flour instead, so they are gluten-free when using certified gluten-free oat flour and rolled oats. It's basically a fistful of muesli . . . right?

Makes: *9 muffins* | Time: *30 min*

Ingredients

- 2 very ripe bananas
- ¼ cup (60 g) plant-based milk e.g. rice milk
- 1 teaspoon coconut oil
- ½ cup (50 g) walnuts
- 6 soft dates
- 1 cup (100 g) oat flour
- 1 teaspoon baking powder
- 1 tablespoon raisins
- 1 tablespoon rolled oats

Instructions

1. Preheat the oven to 360°F/180°C.

2. Peel the bananas and mash them with a fork until puréed. Add the plant-based milk and coconut oil and give it quick mix.

3. Chop the walnuts and soft dates into smaller pieces.

4. In a large mixing bowl, add the oat flour and baking powder and give it a quick whisk. Then, pour in the banana-milk-oil mixture, as well as the raisins, chopped walnuts, and dates and whisk until a creamy batter forms.

5. Scoop the batter into a muffin pan lined with muffin wrappers and sprinkle the rolled oats on top.

6. Bake the muffins for about 15 to 20 minutes, until golden on top and done in the middle. You can use the toothpick method (see Bianca's Kitchen Hack on pg. 165) to make sure your muffins are baked all the way through.

NUTTY CHOCOLATE GRANOLA

This chocolate granola is the ultimate chocolate crunch experience that you can (and should!) enjoy for breakfast. Simply snack on the big chunks or put them in plant-based milk, on yogurt, or nice cream. The possibilities are endless!

Makes: *2 cups* | Time: *25 min*

Instructions

1. Preheat the oven to 360°F/180°C.

2. Pour the liquid coconut oil into a large bowl, add the maple syrup and cocoa powder, and mix well until it resembles melted chocolate.

3. Add in the rolled oats and give it a good mix. Lastly, fold in the chopped chocolate, almonds, and walnuts.

4. Place the mixture on a baking sheet lined with parchment paper and spread it so it's approximately 1-inch thick.

5. Bake in the oven for about 10 to 15 minutes. Let it cool off completely before breaking it in chunks and using it in your breakfast with vegan milk, yogurt, or on nice cream.

6. To store the granola, keep it in an airtight jar at room temperature for up to 3 weeks.

Ingredients

- 1 tablespoon coconut oil, liquid
- 2 tablespoons maple syrup or agave syrup
- 1½ tablespoons cocoa powder
- 1 cup (100g) rolled oats*
- ½ cup (75g) chopped chocolate or semi-sweet chocolate chips
- ½ cup (50g) mix of raw almonds and walnuts, roughly chopped

*Use certified gluten-free oats if you want to make the granola gluten-free.

STRAWBERRY CHIA PUDDING

If you're looking for an easy breakfast that you can prepare the day before, you'll love chia puddings! The best thing is you could also fill them in mason jars and have your versatile, filling breakfast ready to go. With a simple basic formula, you can make endless varieties of chia puddings!

Makes: *2 servings* | Time: *10 min + overnight waiting time*

Ingredients

- 1 cup (150 g) thawed strawberries + more to top the chia pudding
- 1½ cups (360 ml) unsweetened rice milk*
- 2 teaspoons maple syrup
- ½ cup (80 g) chia seeds
- 1 teaspoon coconut flakes

Instructions

1. Place 1 cup of thawed strawberries together with the rice milk and maple syrup in a high-speed blender. Blend until it's a smooth and fine strawberry milk.

2. Fill the strawberry milk mixture in a bowl and add the chia seeds. Give it a good mix and set it aside for about 30 minutes.

3. Mix the chia pudding again and divide it into two glasses. Let it thicken in the fridge for about 4 to 5 hours or overnight.

4. Top the Strawberry Chia Pudding with the rest of the thawed strawberries and sprinkle with coconut flakes before serving.

Bianca's Kitchen Hack
How to Make Chia Pudding

The basic formula for chia puddings is: ¼ cup of chia seeds per 1 cup of liquid.

---

*If you use sweetened rice milk, you can leave out the maple syrup.

PAN-ROASTED TOMATO BRUSCHETTA

This pan-roasted tomato bruschetta is not just a snack to us. We associate this juicy treat with brunch on balconies and the sun on our faces. We highly recommend making this when tomatoes are in season, so that they taste the sweetest and most flavorful.

Makes: *2 large bruschetta breads* | Time: *15 min*

Instructions

1. Wash and halve the cherry tomatoes. Toss them in a pan with the coconut oil—keep on medium to high heat. Start by adding salt, balsamic vinegar, and garlic powder. Keep it on high heat and stir occasionally.

2. In the meantime, toast the white bread slices in a pan, on an electric griller, or in the oven.

3. Once the tomatoes lose most of their water and look good to you, put them on the white bread slices and top with fresh basil. They are best enjoyed fresh and warm, otherwise the bread gets soggy.

Ingredients

20 cherry tomatoes

½ teaspoon coconut oil

1 dash of salt or more, to taste

¼ teaspoon balsamic vinegar

1 pinch of garlic powder

2 large slices white bread (see on pg. 110 for homemade)

½ teaspoon fresh basil, chopped

WAFFLES WITH A WARM RASPBERRY SAUCE

I love making easy, fruity sauces by simply heating up frozen fruits and adding a bit of maple syrup. It's such a marvelous addition to delicious vegan waffles. Oh, and also, here's a waffle recipe.

Makes: *4 waffles* | Time: *30 min*

Instructions for the Raspberry Sauce

1. Heat the frozen raspberries together with the maple syrup in a small pot and let it simmer for about 5 minutes. Mash the raspberries with a fork and let it thicken up a bit.

Instructions for the Waffles

1. In another pot, heat the plant-based milk with the coconut oil until the oil is liquid and warm.

2. Combine the flour, baking powder, sugar, and salt in a mixing bowl. Add the milk and oil mixture and whisk until combined. It should be a thick, sticky batter.

3. Heat the waffle iron and spray it generously with the oil, so that the waffles don't stick to the iron later.

4. Spray a waffle iron or pan with nonstick cooking spray and add about ¼ of the waffle batter for each waffle. Let the waffles cook in the iron or pan until slightly brown on the edges.

5. Once you've made all the waffles, stack them up, spread the warm raspberry sauce on top, and sprinkle with the lemon zest and powdered sugar. Enjoy!

Ingredients for the Raspberry Sauce

¾ cup (75 g) frozen raspberries

1 teaspoon maple syrup

Ingredients for the Waffles

¾ cup (180 ml) plant-based milk e.g. unsweetened rice milk

1 tablespoon coconut oil

1¼ cups (150 g) all-purpose flour

2 teaspoons baking powder

1 tablespoon vegan white sugar

1 pinch of salt

Nonstick cooking spray for the waffle iron

1 teaspoon lemon zest, freshly grated

Powdered sugar for dusting

SOUPS

BROCCOLI SOUP WITH GARLIC CROUTONS

We don't need tons of ingredients for a really good, creamy broccoli soup. The coconut swirls on top are a must-have and the homemade garlic croutons are an excellent crispy addition!

Makes: *2 servings* | Time: *30 min*

Instructions

1. In a large pot, bring the water to a boil.

2. Chop the broccoli into florets, wash them, and add them to the boiling water. Let them cook for about 7 minutes, until softened.

3. Use a slotted spoon to transfer the soft broccoli to a blender and add 2 cups of the broccoli water. Check out Bianca's Kitchen Hack below for how to prevent blended hot liquids from exploding all over your kitchen. Preferably, also let the hot liquid cool down before blending.

4. For the garlic croutons, add olive oil, salt, garlic powder, and bread cubes into a pan and pan-fry the bread cubes until golden on all sides.

5. Blend the broccoli soup until it is completely smooth, add in the coconut milk, parsley, and ½ teaspoon salt + more to taste.

6. Once you're happy with the taste, reheat the soup in the pot, pour it into bowls, add the coconut milk swirls, top with garlic croutons, and serve.

Ingredients for the Broccoli Soup

4 cups (1 liter) water

1 head of broccoli

¼ cup (60 ml) full-fat canned coconut milk + more for swirls

1 small bunch of parsley

½ teaspoon salt + more to taste

Ingredients for the Garlic Croutons

1 teaspoon olive oil

¼ teaspoon salt

¼ teaspoon garlic powder

1½ cups (45g) bread cubes

Bianca's Kitchen Hack
How to Blend Hot Liquids

You can make really easy and delicious creamy soups in a blender. However, be careful when working with hot liquids. Don't fill the blender more than halfway, remove the blender's center lid piece, and hold a kitchen towel over the top. Trust us on this one; we've had soup all over our kitchen walls once. (Well, twice.) Never again.

HEALING LEMON THYME LENTIL SOUP

If you're feeling a cold creeping in, this is the soup you want to make immediately! The immune-boosting powers of thyme, garlic, turmeric, and lemon will give you just the right amount of energy you need to get well soon.

Makes: *4 servings* | Time: *30 min*

Ingredients

- 1 teaspoon olive oil
- 1 red onion, diced
- 2 garlic cloves, minced
- 2 carrots, sliced
- 19 oz. (500 g) canned brown lentils, drained and rinsed
- 1 tablespoon lemon zest
- 1 tablespoon lemon juice + more to taste
- 3 cups (750 ml) water
- 1 teaspoon thyme
- ¼ teaspoon turmeric powder
- ½ teaspoon salt + more to taste
- Fresh parsley for garnish
- Lemon wedges for garnish

Instructions

1. In a large pot, add the olive oil, diced onion, minced garlic, and sliced carrots. Let it cook on medium heat for about 8 to 10 minutes while stirring occasionally until the onion is translucent.

2. Add in the rinsed brown lentils, lemon zest, and lemon juice.

3. Cover with the 3 cups of water, and add in the thyme, turmeric powder, and salt. Bring it to a quick boil and let it simmer for about 15 minutes.

4. Add more salt and lemon juice to taste.

5. Serve and garnish with fresh parsley and a lemon wedge or two.

SOOTHING MUSHROOM RAMEN SOUP WITH CRISPY TOFU

After exhausting days at work, there's only one option that brings us back all the comfort in the world: soup. This is why we came up with this Asian-style mushroom ramen soup. We love the combination of spinach and mushrooms!

Makes: *2 servings* | Time: *25 min*

Instructions

1. In a large pot with sesame oil, add in sliced mushrooms, carrot, and scallion. Add soy sauce and let it cook until the mushrooms have lost most of their water. Then, add in the spinach, water, and 1 tablespoon miso paste. Give it a good mix, and let it cook for about 5 to 10 minutes until the carrots are soft. Set aside.

2. Meanwhile, heat a large pan with the canola oil and season it with the salt and curry powder. Tilt the pan until spices and oil are combined, then add the tofu slices. Cook on medium to high heat for about 8 to 10 minutes until golden brown on one side, then flip and repeat.

3. Add the ramen noodles into the soup for a few minutes until soft. Add more miso paste and soy sauce to taste.

4. Once the ramen noodles are soft, pour the soup into bowls, add the pan-roasted tofu, and top with a few freshly cut scallions.

Ingredients

1 teaspoon sesame oil

3 cups (360 g) mushrooms, sliced

1 large carrot, peeled and sliced

1 scallion, thinly sliced + more for garnish

½ teaspoon soy sauce + more to taste

1 cup (100 g) frozen or 2 cups (200 g) fresh spinach

3 cups (750 ml) water

1 tablespoon miso paste + more to taste

2 teaspoons canola oil

¼ teaspoon salt

¼ teaspoon curry powder

8 slices firm tofu

2 portions (125 g) vegan ramen noodles

RED MUSHROOM SOUP

First things first: obviously there isn't any fly agaric in this soup, as it's poisonous. But this simple tomato soup with coconut milk spots looks just like it and is a cute idea for an easy-to-make, kid-friendly meal.

Makes: *2 servings* | Time: *10 min*

Ingredients

- 2 cups (500 g) tomato passata*
- 1 teaspoon dried basil
- 1 teaspoon dried oregano
- ½ teaspoon salt + more to taste
- ¼ teaspoon garlic powder
- Ground pepper, to taste
- 2 tablespoons coconut milk

Instructions

1. In a pot, heat the tomato passata on medium to low heat until hot. Then, add the herbs and spices. Add more to taste.

2. Transfer the soup into bowls. Carefully drizzle little spots of coconut milk on the soup directly before serving. Enjoy!

*Preferably, use tomato passata consisting of only tomatoes and salt. If it already has herbs added to it, you might want to start with less and add more herbs and spices to taste!

CHEAP AND FILLING POTATO SOUP

A simple potato soup definitely belongs on the list of our favorite soups. With only six ingredients, you'll love this easy-to-make and satisfyingly filling soup. If you're feeling adventurous, you can play around with different veggies as add-ins for the soup.

Makes: *2 servings* | Time: *30 min*

Instructions

1. In a large pot, heat olive oil on medium, add the potatoes, and stir. Let them cook for about 2 minutes, then add veggie broth until the potatoes are covered.

2. Cook on medium to high heat for about 15 minutes with the lid on until the potatoes are soft, and use a potato masher to mash them halfway through. You still want potato bits left in there.

3. Add the carrots and peas and let everything cook for a couple of minutes until the carrots are soft.

4. Add more veggie broth if there isn't enough liquid left. Add fresh rosemary for garnish.

Ingredients

1 teaspoon olive oil

3 cups (500 g) potatoes, peeled and cubed

2 cups (500 ml) veggie broth

3 carrots, peeled and cubed

½ cup (70 g) frozen peas

Fresh rosemary for garnish

Sascha's Landmine Situation
On a Budget

The good news first: I have never heard a longtime vegan complain about how expensive vegan food is. The bad news: it can be if you continuously substitute vegan meat alternatives; they're neither healthy, nor that cheap. As a matter of fact, just a few slices of vegan sausage can often burn a hole in your budget. However, fresh produce, lentils, and tofu don't have to be expensive at all! If you live on a tight budget, you might want to look into cooking in bulk, as most vegan meals are freezer-friendly. Ever checked out the last hour of a farmer's market? Lots of cheap stuff around! Tired of the same, expensive meat alternatives? Try our seitan recipe (see on pg. 21)!

MAIN MEALS

CASHEW PARMESAN PIZZA

Our favorite vegan cheese sauce (see on pg. 18) is amazing on pizza, but a simple roasted veggie pizza with blobs of nut-free arugula pesto and topped with Cashew Parmesan is the perfect alternative if you're looking for a not-too-cheesy pizza.

Makes: *2 pizzas* | Time: *45 min (with the pizza dough ready)*

Ingredients for the Arugula Pesto

- 1½ cups (75 g) arugula
- 1 cup (50 g) basil leaves
- 1 garlic clove, peeled
- ⅓ cup (50 g) sunflower seeds
- 1 tablespoon nutritional yeast
- 2 teaspoons olive oil
- 1 tablespoon lemon juice
- ½ teaspoon salt

Instructions

1. Preheat oven to 480°F/250°C.

2. In a pan with olive oil, cook the onion until translucent on medium heat. Then add in the mushrooms and bell peppers and let it cook until soft. Season with a dash of salt.

3. In a separate bowl, combine the ingredients for the tomato sauce.

4. Divide the Multi-Purpose Bread dough into two equal parts and roll them out on a slightly floured surface. I like to do this on a baking sheet lined with parchment paper. Spread the tomato sauce on top and top with the pan-roasted vegetables and sliced cherry tomatoes.

5. Prepare the arugula pesto by mixing all the ingredients in a food processor until the mixture is combined and fine. Add blobs of arugula pesto onto the pizza.

6. Bake the pizzas in the oven for about 10 to 15 minutes, until the crust is golden and the tomato sauce has thickened.

7. Make sure to sprinkle with Cashew Parmesan before serving!

Ingredients for the Pizza

- 1 teaspoon olive oil
- ½ red onion, sliced
- 1½ cups (180 g) mushrooms, sliced
- 2 red bell peppers, sliced
- 1 dash of salt
- 1 portion of our Multi-Purpose Bread dough (see on pg. 110)
- 5 cherry tomatoes, sliced
- Cashew Parmesan (see on pg. 17) for sprinkling on top

Ingredients for the Tomato Sauce

- ½ cup (125 g) tomato passata
- ½ teaspoon dried basil
- ½ teaspoon dried oregano
- ¼ teaspoon salt
- ⅛ teaspoon garlic powder

AFRICAN-INSPIRED PEANUT BUTTER STEW

A while back, we served this African-inspired peanut butter stew at a party for our friends. Since then, we've been constantly asked to make it again. They asked us to give them our recipe, which we never really did, but all secrets must come to an end—enjoy!

Makes: *4 servings* | Time: *1 hour*

Ingredients

- 1 teaspoon canola oil
- 1 red onion, chopped
- 3 garlic cloves, minced
- 1 cup (160 g) potatoes, chopped
- 1 zucchini, cubed
- 1 carrot, sliced
- 5 cherry tomatoes, halved
- 1 scallion, thinly sliced
- 1 cup (100 g) frozen spinach
- 1/3 cup (80 g) smooth peanut butter
- 2 cups (500 ml) water + more to reach desired consistency
- 1 teaspoon salt
- Roasted peanuts for garnish, chopped
- White rice, for serving

Instructions

1. In a large pot with canola oil, cook the onion and garlic until translucent.

2. Add in the chopped potatoes and let them roast until they turn a nice brownish color.

3. Then, add in the zucchini, carrot, cherry tomatoes, and scallion and let everything cook for a couple of minutes, while stirring occasionally.

4. Then, add the frozen spinach, peanut butter, water, and salt. Let it cook on medium to high heat with the lid on for about 30 minutes. Once the potatoes are soft, the water has cooked down, and the stew has a nice creamy texture, it's ready to serve. If the potatoes are not soft enough but the water has cooked down too much, add ½ cup of water at a time until perfectly creamy.

5. Garnish with roasted peanuts and serve with white rice!

CREAMY AVOCADO PASTA

Pasta in a creamy avocado sauce makes a great and super quick lunch or dinner, which is just as delicious served warm as it is when served cold. No need to heat up the avocado sauce—just toss it in the pasta and it is good to go!

Makes *2 servings* | Time: *15 min*

Instructions

1. Boil the pasta according to package instructions.

2. Meanwhile, add the avocados, lemon juice, basil, garlic powder, 1/3 cup (80 ml) of the pasta water, and salt in a food processor and pulse until a creamy sauce is formed. Add more salt to taste. You may have to scrape down the sides a couple of times.

3. Once the pasta is soft, drain the water and transfer pasta to a large bowl.

4. Add the avocado sauce to the pasta, give it a quick mix, and divide into two bowls.

5. Add the halved cherry tomatoes, sprinkle with Cashew Parmesan, and garnish with fresh basil.

Ingredients

3 cups (300 g) vegan pasta e.g. rotini*

2 avocados, peeled and pitted

2 teaspoons lemon juice

¼ cup (15 g) fresh basil

1 pinch of garlic powder

½ teaspoon salt + more to taste

10 cherry tomatoes, halved

Cashew Parmesan (see on pg. 17)

Fresh basil to garnish

*For a low-carb variation, use spiralized zucchini instead of pasta. Sprinkle the spiralized zucchini with salt, let it sit for 30 minutes, drain it, and your raw zucchini noodles are ready.

CHEESY TEX-MEX WRAPS

These cheesy Tex-Mex wraps filled with rice, corn, kidney beans, lettuce, avocado, and home-made vegan cheese sauce make an awesome and super-filling lunch. They are also great to pack for school or work lunches. Just roll them in parchment paper or aluminum foil to make sure they don't fall apart in transit.

Makes: *4 servings* | Time: *20 min (with the tortilla and cheese sauce ready)*

Ingredients

- 1 teaspoon olive oil
- 1 red onion, chopped
- 2 garlic cloves, minced
- 1 cup (175 g) canned or frozen corn, drained and rinsed
- ¾ cup (115 g) canned kidney beans, drained and rinsed
- Salt, to taste
- Chili powder, to taste
- 1 cup (170 g) cooked rice
- 4 homemade tortillas (see on pg. 118) or store-bought
- 1 cup (50 g) chopped lettuce
- 2 tablespoons cheese sauce (see p. 18)
- 1 avocado, peeled, pitted, cubed
- 1 handful of cherry tomatoes, halved

Instructions

1. In a large pan with a teaspoon of olive oil, cook the chopped red onion and minced garlic on medium heat until translucent. Add the corn and kidney beans, and season with salt and chili powder. Add the cooked rice and give it good mix.

2. Once the veggie rice mixture is warm, start assembling the wraps. On a tortilla, start with lettuce, then add the veggies and rice, drizzle with cheese sauce, and add the cubed avocado and halved cherry tomatoes on top. Roll it up like a burrito and cut in half. Enjoy!

TOMATO COCONUT CHICKPEA CURRY

This is a vegan, gluten-free, creamy, and delicious chickpea curry that's super quick and easy to make. Tomato passata and coconut milk make a great base for curries, and the chickpeas provide this dish with a lot of protein. This curry is best served with homemade naan and basmati rice.

Makes: *2 servings* | Time: *25 min*

Instructions

1. In a large pot with canola oil on medium to high heat, add in the onion, ginger, and garlic. Cook until translucent.

2. Then, add in the chickpeas and curry powder. Let everything cook for about 5 minutes on medium to high heat.

3. Reduce the heat to low and add in the tomato passata, coconut milk, and salt.

4. Stir and let it cook for about 10 minutes (while slowly turning up the heat again). This is the point where you can adjust the curry to your taste by adding more coconut milk, salt, etc. Add cayenne pepper to taste.

5. Once the curry is hot and creamy, transfer it to a bowl, garnish with chopped cilantro, and serve with basmati rice and garlic flatbread.

Ingredients

1 teaspoon canola oil

1 red onion, chopped

½-inch ginger root, minced

3 garlic cloves, minced

1½ cups (260 g) canned chickpeas, drained and rinsed

¼ teaspoon curry powder

1½ cups (375 g) tomato passata*

¼ cup (65 g) full-fat coconut milk

¼ teaspoon salt + more to taste

Cayenne pepper, to taste

Chopped cilantro for garnish

*We used store-bought tomato passata (with salt and no additional herbs) for this recipe; it's often canned or in cartons, not to be confused with tomato paste, which is thicker in consistency. You can also use canned crushed tomatoes instead.

CURRIED COUSCOUS SALAD TO GO

This is a quick and easy recipe for a curried couscous salad to go. Put the different layers for the salad in a sealable mason jar and it's the perfect lunch to take to school, work, or on a picnic!

Makes: *3 servings* | Time: *30 min*

Ingredients for Curried Couscous

- ¾ cup (180 ml) water
- ¼ teaspoon salt
- ½ teaspoon lemon juice
- ½ teaspoon mild curry powder
- ½ cup (90 g) couscous

Ingredients for Crispy Tofu

- 1 tablespoon all-purpose flour
- ¼ teaspoon salt
- ¼ teaspoon paprika powder
- ½ block firm tofu
- 2 teaspoons olive oil

Additional Ingredients

- 6 tablespoons hummus (see on pg. 128) or store-bought
- ½ cup (75 g) chopped cucumber
- A handful of cherry tomatoes per jar, halved
- 1 tablespoon freshly chopped parsley

Instructions

1. Heat the water for the couscous in a large pot. Add the salt, lemon juice, and mild curry powder. When it's boiling, remove the pot from the stovetop. Pour in the couscous and cover with the lid. Let it soak for 3 to 4 minutes until the couscous is done and ready.

2. For the crispy tofu, combine the all-purpose flour with the salt and paprika powder in a large mixing bowl. Cut the tofu into small cubes and toss it in the flour mixture. Give the bowl a good shake until the tofu is coated equally. Heat a large pan with the olive oil and add the tofu as soon as the oil gets hot. Let it cook for a couple of minutes on medium to high heat until the tofu is brown on all sides.

3. Now, let's assemble! Make the hummus the bottom layer so it doesn't soak up the couscous. Then, add the cucumber cubes and halved cherry tomatoes, followed by the curried couscous, then the crispy tofu cubes. Garnish with freshly chopped parsley, and you're good to go.

Sascha's Landmine Situation
When Sudden Cravings Strike

Sudden cravings for meat and cheese are the worst. They're sneaky, unpredictable, and can end in a whole lot of self-doubt. It's okay to have these cravings. What I learned to do is to always have some kind of snack around that reminds you of the dishes you crave. Keep vegan pizza or a batch of your favorite vegan chili in your freezer. If everything fails and you are really urging to fall back into your old ways, remember to make a decision, and make it a conscious one. Hold yourself accountable, because in the end, you are the one who gets to decide if or how you want to label yourself.

EVEN-BETTER-WHEN-REHEATED CHILI SIN CARNE

You can't go wrong with a big pot of chili. Not only do we love to make a big pot of chili just for ourselves, we also love to serve it at parties, because it can easily be reheated, it's super filling and nutritious, and it gets you ready for a long night. The cocoa powder gives it a lovely dark color and adds that special twist. And the best thing—it basically cooks itself.

Makes: *3 servings* | Time: *60 min*

Instructions

1. In a big pot with the olive oil, add the chopped onions and minced garlic. Let it cook on medium heat for a few minutes until translucent.

2. Add in the rinsed and drained corn and kidney beans, water, paprika powder, salt, chili powder, cocoa powder, and tomato passata. Give it a quick stir, put the lid on, and let it cook for about 30 minutes on medium heat. It should thicken quite nicely, and if the water has cooked down too much, you can add more water or tomato passata. Let it cook without the lid on for another 5 to 10 minutes, until it has reached the right consistency.

3. Peel and pit the avocado and cut it in cubes, and top the chili with it. Serve with corn tortilla chips.

Ingredients

1 teaspoon olive oil

2 red onions, chopped

4 garlic cloves, minced

15 oz. (425 g) canned corn, rinsed and drained

15 oz. (425 g) canned kidney beans, rinsed and drained

2 cups (500 ml) water

1 teaspoon paprika powder

1 teaspoon salt + more to taste

1 teaspoon chili powder + more to taste

2 teaspoons cocoa powder

1 cup (250 g) tomato passata

1 avocado

Corn tortilla chips for serving

CARIBBEAN-INSPIRED COCONUT MILK CURRY

This simple coconut milk curry is one of the easiest, quickest, and most nutritious ways to use up all of your leftover veggies. Feel free to add anything your heart desires, such as tofu, cauliflower, or peanuts. We are big fans of the sweet potato and broccoli combination, so that's what we used in this recipe.

Makes: *2 servings* | Time: *30 min*

Ingredients

- 1 small sweet potato, peeled and cubed
- ¼ head of broccoli, cut in florets
- 1 teaspoon olive oil
- ½ red onion, diced
- 2 garlic cloves, minced
- ½-inch ginger root, minced
- ⅓ zucchini, cubed
- ½ red bell pepper, cut in strips
- 2 carrots, peeled and sliced
- 1 shallot, thinly sliced
- ¼ teaspoon salt + more to taste
- ¼ teaspoon curry powder
- Cayenne pepper to taste
- 1 cup (250 ml) full-fat coconut milk
- 2 servings of cooked white rice

Instructions

1. In a large pot with water, boil the sweet potato while steaming the broccoli florets on top in a small colander or steamer basket until the sweet potato is soft. Drain the sweet potato and broccoli and set aside.

2. In a separate pan, cook the red onion, garlic, and ginger in olive oil until translucent.

3. Then, add in the zucchini, bell pepper, carrots, and shallot. Season with ¼ teaspoon salt and let it cook on medium heat until the vegetables are soft.

4. Add curry powder, cayenne pepper, and coconut milk and let it cook further on medium heat for a couple of minutes until the coconut milk thickens.

5. Serve over white rice and enjoy!

BAKED FALAFEL PITA

These baked falafel are the perfect healthy alternative to the usual fried kind. Drizzled with our homemade tahini maple dressing (see on pg. 156) and served with salad, tomatoes, and cucumbers in a warm and fluffy soft pita, this is the lunch you'll want to eat every day.

Makes: *7 pitas* | Time: *1 hour*

Instructions

1. Preheat the oven to 400°F/200°C.

2. Add the chickpeas to a food processor and process for a few seconds until mostly broken up but not totally creamy. (You don't want to make hummus.) Transfer the chickpeas into a large bowl.

3. Then, process the garlic cloves, red onion, and fresh parsley in the food processor until small. Add them to the bowl with the chickpeas.

4. Season with salt and lemon juice and give it a good mix.

5. Add in the canola oil and all-purpose flour into the mix until you can form little patties.

6. Place the falafel patties on a baking tray lined with parchment paper. Spray them with oil.

7. Bake them in the oven for about 30 minutes, flipping them once after about 20 minutes. They should be golden and crispy on the outside and soft but not mushy on the inside.

8. Warm the pitas in a pan or oven, slice them open, fill them with a few salad leaves, cucumber slices, falafel, and cherry tomatoes and drizzle with our Tahini Maple Dressing. Enjoy!

9. If you don't use the falafel all at once, store them in the fridge and reheat them in a pan with olive oil to make them warm and crispy again. You can also freeze them for up to three months!

Ingredients for the Falafel

17 oz. (480 g) canned chickpeas, drained and rinsed

2 garlic cloves, peeled

1 red onion, peeled

¼ cup (15 g) fresh parsley

1 teaspoon salt

1 teaspoon lemon juice

1 teaspoon canola oil

⅓ cup (40g) all-purpose flour or more until the mixture holds together

Nonstick cooking spray

Additional Ingredients

7 pitas

A handful of green salad leaves

¼ cucumber, sliced

A handful of cherry tomatoes, quartered

¼ cup tahini maple dressing (see on pg. 156)

STEAMING HOT VEGGIE LASAGNA

Homemade steaming hot lasagna brings a level of comfort that can hardly be found in any other dish. This lasagna is loaded with veggies such as zucchini, carrots, mushrooms, spinach, and topped with our favorite vegan cheese sauce (see on pg. 18)!

Makes: *6 servings* | Time: *50 min*

Ingredients

- 1 teaspoon olive oil + more to brush the pan
- 1 red onion, diced
- 2 garlic cloves, minced
- 1 zucchini, cubed
- 2½ cups (300 g) sliced mushrooms
- 1 pinch of salt + more to taste
- 3 carrots, grated
- 3 cups (750 g) tomato passata or canned crushed tomatoes
- 1 teaspoon dried basil
- 1 teaspoon dried oregano
- 2 large handfuls fresh spinach
- 12 egg-free ready-to-bake lasagna sheets
- 1 portion of cheese sauce (see on pg. 18)
- Fresh oregano for garnish

Instructions

1. Preheat the oven to 400°F/200°C.

2. In a large pot, heat the olive oil and toss in the chopped red onion and minced garlic. Cook on medium heat until translucent.

3. Then, add the cubed zucchini, mushroom slices, and pinch of salt and cook until the veggies are tender.

4. Then, add in the grated carrots, tomato passata, dried basil, and oregano. Give it a good mix. Add the spinach and let it all cook until the spinach is wilted. Add salt to taste.

5. Let's layer our lasagna! Lightly oil a 7 x 10-inch baking pan with olive oil. Start with a layer of tomato sauce, then some lasagna sheets (for our 7 x 10-inch pan, we use 3 sheets per layer), sauce again, lasagna sheets, and repeat until you've used up all the sauce. Finish by spreading a final layer of sauce on top.

6. Pour the cheese sauce on top and spread it, so the top is completely covered in cheese.

7. Bake the lasagna for about 20 to 25 minutes until the cheese is golden and has brown, crispy spots.

8. Garnish with fresh oregano and enjoy!

LEFTOVER ROASTED VEGGIES

You've probably had this problem before—leftover vegetables in your fridge that are nearing the end of their lifespans. So, let's make use of those sad little veggies that didn't make it into the pot earlier and give them a comeback of the best possible kind! This is our favorite combination, but you can use whatever vegetables you have at home. It will taste different every time!

Makes: *2 servings* | Time: *50 min*

Instructions

1. Preheat the oven to 400°F/200°C.

2. Wash the veggies. Remove the outer leaves of the Brussels sprouts and cut them in half. Cut the eggplant, fennel, red onion, and potatoes in large chunks of similar size. Put all the veggies in a bowl, drizzle with olive oil, and season with salt and dried rosemary.

3. Transfer the veggies to a baking tray lined with parchment paper and make sure they are spread evenly.

4. Bake in the oven for about 20 minutes or until the first veggies start turning a brown color, and flip them over to bake them evenly. If the veggies look dry to you, add another drizzle of olive oil. Bake for another 20 minutes or so, until the potatoes are soft inside and crisp around the edges.

5. Sprinkle with more salt to taste after baking, and serve.

Ingredients

2 cups (200 g) Brussels sprouts

½ eggplant

1 fennel bulb

1 large red onion

5 medium potatoes

1 tablespoon olive oil

½ teaspoon salt + more to taste

½ teaspoon dried rosemary

MAC & CHEESE & PEAS

This is our take on the classic mac & cheese. For the cheese, we're using our basic vegan cheese sauce made out of nutritional yeast. The crispy panko surface adds a lovely crunch! Of course, you can always swap the peas with your favorite vegetable or leave them out completely if you're feeling naughty.

Makes: *2–3 servings* | Time: *35 min*

Ingredients

- 1½ cups (150 g) elbow macaroni pasta, uncooked
- ⅓ cup (50 g) frozen peas
- ⅓ cup (20 g) Panko breadcrumbs
- ¼ teaspoon salt
- ½ teaspoon dried parsley
- ¼ teaspoon garlic powder
- ¼ teaspoon onion powder
- 1 portion of the cheese sauce (see on pg. 18)
- Nonstick cooking spray

Instructions

1. Boil the pasta until soft and steam the frozen peas in a small sieve on top of the pasta until soft.

2. Preheat the oven to 400°F/200°C.

3. In a separate bowl, mix the Panko breadcrumbs with the salt and dried parsley.

4. Drain the pasta (reserve ¼ cup of the cooking water for later, to thin out the cheese sauce) and put the pasta back into the pot. Add in the peas, garlic powder, onion powder, and cheese sauce. Then, add in the reserved cooking water and give it a quick mix.

5. Transfer the mac & cheese to a lightly oiled oven-safe 5 x 8-inch pan and sprinkle with the spiced Panko breadcrumbs. Spray the top of the mac & cheese with the cooking spray, and put it in the oven for about 5 to 10 minutes until it gets a nice and brown on top.

MIDDLE EASTERN-INSPIRED EGGPLANT WITH RAISIN WALNUT RICE

This baked eggplant served over a raisin walnut rice is inspired by Middle Eastern cuisine. Instead of baking the eggplant in the oven, you could also grill it in the summer! It's such a good-looking dish, isn't it?

Makes: *2 servings* | Time: *45 min*

Instructions

1. Preheat the oven to 400°F/200°C.

2. Wash the eggplants and cut it in half lengthwise. Carefully cut a diamond pattern in each eggplant half.

3. Combine the oil with the salt, thyme, white sesame seeds, and lemon zest. Brush the eggplant halves with this mixture and place them flesh-side up on a baking sheet lined with parchment paper. Bake for about 30 to 45 minutes until soft and golden on top.

4. For the raisin walnut rice, heat olive oil in a pan, add in the walnuts and raisins, and let it cook on medium heat for 2 to 3 minutes. Then, add in the cooked rice and add salt to taste. Let it cook for a few minutes until warm.

5. For serving, top the raisin walnut rice with the eggplant halves and garnish with fresh parsley.

Ingredients for the Eggplant

2 eggplants

1 tablespoon olive oil

½ teaspoon salt

1 teaspoon thyme

¼ teaspoon white sesame seeds

2 teaspoons lemon zest

Fresh parsley for garnish

Ingredients for the Raisin Walnut Rice

1 teaspoon olive oil

⅓ cup (35 g) walnuts, chopped

¼ cup (45 g) raisins

2 cups (340 g) cooked rice

Salt to taste

PENNE RATATOUILLE

Penne ratatouille is one of our favorite go-to-meals. With the eggplant, cherry tomatoes, zucchini, red pepper, and canned artichokes, you'll get a huge portion of veggies in your meal—combined with delicious pasta.

Makes: *2 servings* | Time: *40 min*

Ingredients

- 2 cups (200 g) penne pasta, uncooked
- 2 teaspoons canola oil
- ½ red onion, chopped
- 2 garlic cloves, thinly sliced
- ⅓ eggplant, cubed
- ½ zucchini, cubed
- 1 red bell pepper, cubed
- ¼ teaspoon salt + more to taste
- 4 canned artichoke halves, cubed
- 10 cherry tomatoes, halved
- 1½ cups (375 g) tomato passata
- Cashew Parmesan (see on pg. 17), fresh basil, and oregano for garnish

Instructions

1. Cook the pasta according to package instructions in a large pot with water.

2. In a large pan with canola oil, cook onion and garlic on medium heat for 4 to 5 minutes until translucent. Add the cubed eggplant, zucchini, bell pepper, and salt. Let it cook on medium to high until softened. Add artichokes and cherry tomatoes and let everything cook for another 5 minutes until softened, stirring occasionally.

3. Once all of the veggies are soft, reduce the heat a bit and add the tomato passata. Give it a quick stir, cook until hot, and add more salt to taste.

4. When the penne is done cooking, drain it, add it to the sauce, and stir. Make sure everything's hot before serving. Garnish with our homemade Cashew Parmesan, fresh basil, and oregano.

Bianca's Kitchen Hack
How to Prevent Overboiling

A simple trick to prevent overboiling, especially if you're like me and always get distracted while cooking, is to put a large wooden spoon over the top of the pot. This will pop the bubbles and prevent the water from boiling over as quickly.

STOVETOP AVOCADO PIZZA

Sometimes you just don't have the time, patience, or motivation to make a yeasty pizza dough. This no-yeast, no-bake, stovetop pizza dough is the perfect substitute for that. Topped with mashed avocados and roasted cherry tomatoes, it will satisfy all your pizza cravings without missing any cheese!

Makes: *2 pizzas* | Time: *25 min*

Instructions

1. For a quick yeast-free pizza dough, combine the all-purpose flour, baking powder, and salt in a large bowl. Add the olive oil and water (little by little) and knead until a smooth dough firms. Note that you may not need all the water, or you may have to add a bit more to get a smooth, non-sticky dough. If the dough becomes too sticky, add a bit more flour. You can either knead it by hand or in a stand mixer.

2. Divide the dough into two pieces and roll them out on a floured surface. Put one pizza dough in a really hot flat pan for 1 to 2 minutes until golden on the bottom. Then, flip and let the other side get golden, as well. Repeat for the other pizza.

3. Mash the avocados and mix them with lemon juice and salt in a bowl.

4. Roast the cherry tomato halves in a pan with olive oil on medium to high heat for a couple of minutes until warm, soft, and with a few brown spots. Add 1 splash of balsamic vinegar.

5. Spread the avocado mash on the pizza and top with the roasted cherry tomatoes. Add freshly ground pepper on top and enjoy!

Ingredients for the Yeast-Free Pizza Dough

- 2½ cups (300 g) all-purpose flour
- 1 tablespoon baking powder
- 1 teaspoon salt
- 1 teaspoon olive oil
- 2/3 cup (160 ml) lukewarm water

Ingredients for the Toppings

- 2 avocados, peeled, pitted
- ½ teaspoon lemon juice
- ¼ teaspoon salt
- 12 cherry tomatoes, halved
- 1 teaspoon olive oil
- 1 splash of balsamic vinegar
- Freshly ground pepper to taste

SUSHI BOWL WITH SESAME-CRUSTED TOFU

A deconstructed sushi bowl makes a delicious and filling lunch that is great to take to work, school, or a picnic. You can't go wrong with veggies, tofu, or whatever you want on a bed of delicious rice. This recipe is also great to make if you don't have the skill or patience to make your own sushi. You can play around with different toppings such as avocado, pumpkin, soybean sprouts, radish, or whatever you feel like.

Makes: *2 bowls* | Time: *1 hour + time to let the rice cool down*

Ingredients for Sushi Rice

- 1 cup (200 g) sushi rice or short-grain rice
- 1½ cups (360 ml) water
- ½ teaspoon salt
- ½ teaspoon brown rice vinegar

Ingredients for Sesame-Crusted Tofu

- 7 oz. (200g) firm tofu
- 3 tablespoons all-purpose flour, divided
- 2 tablespoons water
- 3 tablespoons white sesame seeds
- ¾ teaspoon salt
- 2 teaspoons canola oil

Instructions

1. Wash the rice until the water stays clear and cook the rice according to package instructions. Season with salt and brown rice vinegar and let the rice cool down.

2. Meanwhile, cut the firm tofu in cubes. Combine 1 tablespoon all-purpose flour and the water for the batter in a bowl. In another bowl, combine the white sesame seeds, 2 tablespoons of all-purpose flour, and salt to make the coating. Work in batches to coat the tofu cubes first in the wet batter, then transfer it into the dry coating, and shake carefully so the tofu is coated evenly. Repeat until all of the tofu cubes are coated. Heat enough oil in a pan to cover the bottom. Once hot, add in the tofu cubes and pan-fry them on medium-high heat until crispy. Turn the tofu cubes over and let them get crispy on all sides. Set them aside.

3. In the same pan, quickly pan-roast the soy beans with lemon juice and add salt to taste.

4. Once everything's ready, you can start assembling your sushi bowl.

5. Cover the bottom of your bowl with sushi rice and place the carrot, scallion, cucumber, nori strips, sesame crusted tofu, soy beans, and pickled ginger on top. Sprinkle black sesame seeds on top.

Continued on next page

Additional Ingredients

- ½ cup (50 g) fresh green soy beans
- ½ teaspoon lemon juice
- 1 carrot, peeled and julienned
- ½ scallion, thinly sliced
- ¼ cucumber, julienned
- ¼ nori sheet, cut in strips
- 2 tablespoons pickled ginger
- 1 teaspoon black sesame seeds

VEGGIE STIR-FRY WITH PEANUT BUTTER SAUCE

A simple veggie stir-fry served over white rice is one of our favorite go-to we-don't-know-what-to-cook meals. This version is topped with a creamy peanut butter sauce and roasted, crushed peanuts, which take this dish to the next level. To mix things up, you can use different veggies or serve it over noodles!

Makes: *2 servings* | Time: *45 min*

Instructions

1. In a large pan, heat 1 teaspoon of olive oil and cook the diced onion, minced garlic, and ginger on medium heat until translucent. Transfer the onion, garlic, and ginger to a bowl and set aside.

2. In the same pan, add in the broccoli and cook on low heat until almost soft.

3. Add the cubed zucchini and eggplant to the broccoli and season with the salt to help it draw water out of vegetables. Let them cook on medium to high heat while stirring occasionally. If they stick to the pan, add the remaining teaspoon of olive oil.

4. Once the zucchini and eggplant are soft, add the carrot, red bell pepper, and shallot and let them cook for about 5 minutes until the carrot has softened. Then, add in the onion, garlic, and ginger and give everything a good mix. Season with more salt to taste.

5. Add hot water to the peanut butter and whisk until it reaches a creamy and pourable consistency. (The amount of water you need can vary based on the peanut butter you're using and where you're storing it. I typically add in ¼ cup of hot water because I store my peanut butter in the fridge and it gets quite solid. If you store your peanut butter at room temperature, you may need less water.) Then, add the soy sauce and whisk again.

6. Serve the stir-fry over white rice, top with the peanut butter sauce, and garnish with roasted, crushed peanuts.

Ingredients for the Stir-Fry

2 teaspoons olive oil, divided

½ red onion, diced

1 garlic clove, minced

½-inch ginger root, minced

½ broccoli, cut in small florets

½ teaspoon salt + more to taste

1 zucchini, cubed

½ eggplant, cubed

1 carrot, peeled and sliced

1 red bell pepper, sliced

1 shallot, thinly sliced

Ingredients for the Peanut Butter Sauce

¼ cup hot water to thin out the sauce

2 tablespoons peanut butter

¼ teaspoon soy sauce

Additional Ingredients

Roasted peanuts for garnish, crushed

2 servings of cooked white rice

SPAGHETTI CARROT BOLOGNESE

When we're undecided on what to eat, we usually make this simple spaghetti carrot Bolognese, because it's made with simple ingredients we almost always have at home. it's also a real comfort food for us. Topped with our homemade Cashew Parmesan, it's quite the fancy date night dinner!

Makes: *2 servings* | Time: *30 min*

Ingredients

3 large carrots

3 garlic cloves

1 red onion

4 oz. (150 g) spaghetti noodles

1 teaspoon olive oil

1½ cups (375 g) tomato passata or canned crushed tomatoes

¾ teaspoon dried basil

¾ teaspoon dried oregano

¾ teaspoon salt + more to taste

Cashew Parmesan (see pg. 17)

Fresh basil for garnish

Instructions

1. Peel the carrots, garlic, and onion. Cut the carrots in large chunks and chop together with the onion and garlic in a food processor until fine.

2. Boil the spaghetti noodles according to package instructions.

3. While the spaghetti is cooking, heat olive oil in a separate pot with the chopped onion, garlic, and carrots and cook for 4 to 5 minutes until the onion is translucent.

4. Then, add the tomato passata, herbs, and salt. Let the carrot Bolognese cook for about 10 to 15 minutes.

5. Serve and garnish with Cashew Parmesan and fresh basil.

SWEET POTATO HAWAII BURGER

Bring some summer feeling into your kitchen with these sweet potato Hawaii burgers. The sweet potato in the patty and the roasted pineapple add a lovely sweet touch, while the arugula balances everything out quite nicely.

Makes: *4 burgers* | Time: *1 hour (with the burger buns ready)*

Instructions

1. Boil sweet potatoes until soft.

2. Preheat oven to 400°F/200°C.

3. Add the cooked sweet potato in a bowl and mash. Add the sunflower seeds, rolled oats, parsley, and salt. Mix well. Let the mixture cool off until cold enough to handle.

4. Form 4 patties and transfer them to a baking tray lined with parchment paper. Spray with oil.

5. Bake in the oven for about 30 minutes, flipping them once after 15 minutes.

6. Grill the pineapple in an electric grill or in a pan.

7. Add arugula to the burger bun, followed by the sweet potato patty and grilled pineapple.

Ingredients for the patty

- 1 (1½ cups or 200 g) sweet potato, peeled, cubed
- ⅓ cup (45 g) sunflower seeds
- ½ cup (50 g) rolled oats
- 1 tablespoon fresh parsley
- ½ teaspoon salt
- Nonstick cooking spray

Additional Ingredients

- 4 slices of canned pineapple
- 1 cup (50 g) arugula
- 4 homemade burger buns (see on pg. 110) or store-bought

Bianca's Kitchen Hack
How to Make Burger Patties that Don't Fall Apart

For years, I've had problems making good burger patties that stick together. But then I found the magic component: rolled oats. Use a creamy mashed veggie base, sweet potatoes, white potatoes, or black beans and combine them with rolled oats, as they act as a great binder. I also like to add nuts or sunflower seeds for some texture. Don't forget to add lots of spices!

TOTALLY UNAUTHENTIC PAELLA

We claim no authenticity for this paella, but it is delicious and looks super fancy! Thanks to the saffron, this dish gets its typical yellow-orange color and unique taste. Due to the saltiness of the dried tomatoes, olives, and veggie broth, no additional salt is needed.

Makes: *2–3 servings* | Time: *45 min*

Ingredients

- 1 teaspoon olive oil
- 1 red onion, diced
- 2 garlic cloves, minced
- ½ zucchini, cubed
- ½ red bell pepper, cubed
- 4 dried tomatoes, cut in small pieces
- ½ cup (65 g) pitted green olives, halved
- 1 cup (200 g) short grain rice
- 2 cups (480 ml) veggie broth
- ⅛ teaspoon saffron
- Lemon wedges and fresh parsley for garnish

Instructions

1. Heat the olive oil in a large (9-inch) pan and cook the onion and garlic until translucent.

2. Then, add in the cubed zucchini and red bell pepper and let it cook for a few minutes until softened.

3. Add the dried tomatoes and green olives and give it a quick mix.

4. Add the short grain rice, veggie broth, and saffron and mix everything together. The rice should be covered with water.

5. Let it cook on medium heat without a lid for about 20 minutes until the rice has absorbed the water.

6. Before serving, add lemon wedges and fresh parsley on top, and enjoy!

QUICK VEGGIE FAJITAS

Roasted veggies combined with a guacamole-like avocado sauce in soft wheat tortillas are an easy and heavenly way to treat yourself to some more vegetables. It's an excellent light lunch for sunny days and makes for a great take-to-work lunch when folded into a burrito.

Makes: *4 fajitas* | Time: *25 min*

Instructions

1. In a large pan, heat the olive oil and cook the diced onion and minced garlic on medium heat until translucent.

2. Add the mushrooms, red and green bell peppers, and zucchini. Season with ½ teaspoon salt and ½ teaspoon thyme and let it cook on medium heat until soft while stirring occasionally.

3. In a bowl, mash the avocados with a fork and add the lemon juice and salt. Mix well.

4. In a hot pan, quickly heat the tortillas until warm. Then, spread about a tablespoon of avocado sauce on top of each tortilla, top with roasted veggies, fold it in, and enjoy!

Ingredients

1 teaspoon olive oil

½ red onion, diced

2 garlic cloves, minced

2 cups (240 g) mushrooms, sliced

1 red bell pepper, sliced

1 green bell pepper, sliced

½ zucchini, cut in sticks

1 teaspoon salt, divided

½ teaspoon dried thyme

2 ripe avocados, peeled and pitted

1 teaspoon lemon juice

4 homemade tortillas (see on pg. 118) or store-bought

BREADS

MULTI-PURPOSE BREAD

Have you ever wanted to have one dough recipe that you can use for everything? One simple and delicious recipe to perfect and reuse for all your bready needs? With this basic dough recipe, your dreams will come true. You'll be able to make homemade white bread, naan, pretzel bites, breadsticks, burger buns, pizza, and so much more. We use this Multi-Purpose Bread dough for a couple of recipes in this cookbook (see on pg. 65. 113, 141). In these cases, prepare the bread according to instructions 1–3, work more flour into the dough after it doubles in size, and mold the dough into whatever shape your recipe calls for (buns, pizzas, breadsticks, etc.).

Makes: *1 loaf, 4 buns, 2 pizzas, 16 breadsticks, etc.* | Time: *20 min + 2½ hours rising time*

Ingredients

- 2½ cups (300 g) all-purpose flour
- 1 teaspoon active dry yeast
- ¾ cup (180 ml) lukewarm water, divided
- ½ teaspoon salt
- 1 teaspoon olive oil

Instructions

1. Add the flour in a large mixing bowl, make a well in the middle, and add in the yeast and ¼ cup water. Let it rest for about 10 minutes. If the yeast gets bubbly, you can be sure it's working.

2. Add in the salt, oil, and remaining water. Combine all ingredients with a large spoon, then knead by hand until a soft dough firms or put all the ingredients in a bread baking machine and let the machine knead the dough.

3. Cover the bowl of dough with a clean kitchen towel in a warm spot and let it sit for 1½ to 2 hours until the dough doubles in size.

4. Preheat the oven to 480°F/250°C.

5. Add more flour to the dough and work it into the dough until it's smooth and nonsticky. Transfer the dough to a baking tray lined with lightly floured parchment paper, and form a loaf.

6. Carve the surface of the dough lightly with a knife (we make one long cut across the bread).

7. Then, bake the bread in the oven for 25 to 30 minutes and take it out when the surface is golden. The bread is done when you can knock on the bottom and it sounds hollow.

Bianca's Kitchen Hack
How to Make Seeds Stick to Buns

If poppy seeds or sesame seeds don't want to stick to your burger buns, brush the top with water or plant-based milk and then apply the seeds. The flour in the buns and the water will act like a glue. If you want to add seeds after baking, I recommend using water and a bit of maple syrup to make the top sticky enough.

ENGLISH MUFFINS

This is a super simple recipe for English muffins using only six ingredients. They are fluffy and soft on the inside, and perfect for Saturday mornings. You can also prepare them on the weekend, and enjoy them warm and freshly toasted on weekday mornings. We prefer ours simple—with just a bit of vegan butter and a pinch of salt.

Makes: *8 English muffins* | Time: *30 min + 2 hours rising time*

Instructions

1. Follow the first three steps of our Multi-Purpose Bread recipe (see on pg. 110).

2. Divide the dough into 8 equal pieces and form little balls by pinching the ends together. Sprinkle the cornmeal on a parchment paper, place the dough on top, press them down a bit, and flip over, so they're dusted with cornmeal on both sides.

3. Heat a pan, griddle, or skillet on low to medium heat and add the English muffins. Make sure you don't place them too close or they'll stick together.

4. Let them cook on each side for about 5 to 6 minutes. You can adjust the heat as you need to. They should be cooked through but brown on the outside.

5. The English muffins are best served warm. Slice them up and toast on the inside before eating them. Enjoy!

Ingredients

- 1 portion dough (see our Multi-Purpose Bread recipe on pg. 110)
- 1 tablespoon fine cornmeal

CILANTRO FLATBREAD

If you're making a curry and looking for a quick and easy flatbread recipe, this is it! It's made without yeast, which means no long waiting time for the dough to rise! For variation, add garlic or sesame seeds instead of cilantro.

Makes: *2 flatbreads* | Time: *25 min*

Ingredients

- 1 cup (120 g) all-purpose flour + more until a smooth dough forms
- ½ teaspoon salt
- 1 teaspoon baking powder
- 1 teaspoon olive oil
- ½ cup (120 ml) water
- 2 teaspoons melted coconut oil
- 1 tablespoon cilantro, chopped

Instructions

1. Mix the flour, salt, and baking powder in a bowl.

2. Then, add the olive oil and water and combine with a large spoon until a soft dough forms.

3. Now, add more flour and knead it into the dough until the surface is nonsticky.

4. Cover the bowl with a clean kitchen towel and let the dough rest for about 15 minutes.

5. Divide the dough in two portions and roll each one out on a floured surface.

6. Prepare a very hot flat pan—a crepe pan works best—and add each flatbread one at a time. Turn once when there are bubbles on the surface and brown spots on the bottom. Let it cook on the other side until brown spots form.

7. Brush the flatbread with melted coconut oil and sprinkle chopped cilantro on top.

SUNFLOWER & FLAXSEED BREAD

If you're looking for a healthy, nutritious, and flavorful bread, look no further. Anise, cumin, fennel, and coriander seeds are typical flavors for whole wheat bread. As an intriguing extra, the sunflower and flaxseeds give the bread a crunch that will keep you coming back for one last bite.

Makes: *1 loaf* | Time: *1 hour + 2 hours rising time*

Instructions

1. In a large mixing bowl, combine the whole wheat flour and salt, make a well in the middle, and add in the yeast and ¼ cup water. Let it rest for about 10 minutes. If the yeast gets bubbly, you can be sure the yeast is working.

2. Crush the anise, cumin, fennel, and coriander seeds in a mortar.

3. Add in crushed seeds, sunflower seeds, and flaxseeds and give it a quick mix. Then, add in the olive oil and remaining water and mix with a large spoon until combined, then use your hands to knead it until it all comes together. Alternatively, you could throw all of the ingredients in a bread maker and let it do its magic.

4. Cover the bowl of dough with a clean kitchen towel in a warm spot and let it sit for 1½ to 2 hours until the dough doubles in size.

5. Preheat the oven to 400°F/200 °C.

6. Transfer the dough to a lightly oiled loaf pan and spread it evenly. Add a few more sunflower seeds on top.

7. Bake the bread in the oven for about 40 minutes and take it out once the surface is golden. The bread is done when you can knock on the bottom and it sounds hollow.

Ingredients

- 2½ cups (300 g) whole wheat flour
- ½ teaspoon salt
- 1 teaspoon active dry yeast
- 1 cup (240 ml) water, divided
- 2 teaspoons anise seeds
- 2 teaspoons cumin seeds
- 2 teaspoons fennel seeds
- 2 teaspoons coriander seeds
- ½ cup (70 g) sunflower seeds + more to sprinkle on top
- ¼ cup (40 g) flaxseeds
- 1 teaspoon olive oil

BETTER-THAN-STORE-BOUGHT TORTILLAS

A little warning: once you start making your own tortillas from scratch, you'll never want to go back to the store-bought kind! They are much more filling, and it just feels good and is extremely rewarding to know that you've made them yourself. Plus, you can make them super thick and fluffy by making them smaller and thicker in size.

Makes: *4 tortillas* | Time: *20 min + 2 hours rising time*

Ingredients

- 1²/₃ cups (200 g) all-purpose flour and extra for dusting
- 1²/₃ cups (200 g) spelt flour
- 2 teaspoons active dry yeast
- ½ teaspoon salt
- 2 teaspoons olive oil
- ¾ cup (180 ml) water

Instructions

1. In a mixing bowl, add the dry ingredients first and give it a mix. Pour in the oil and add the water little by little and knead the dough by hand or use a stand mixer until smooth. Add more water or flour if necessary—the dough should be a smooth, nonsticky consistency.

2. Cover the bowl with a clean kitchen towel and let it rest in a warm place for about 1 to 2 hours. The dough should double in size.

3. Punch the dough down a bit, and cut it in 4 equal pieces.

4. Form the pieces into balls and roll them out on a floured surface.

5. Put one tortilla in a very hot, nonstick pan (a flat pan like a crepe pan works best) and place it in there for a few seconds to a minute, then turn when the tortilla is getting bubbly on the surface. Repeat for the other tortillas.

6. Keep the tortillas covered with a clean kitchen towel until serving to prevent them from drying out.

SNACKS & PARTY FOOD

LAST-MINUTE GUACAMOLE

Can a party without guacamole really be considered a party? We don't think so! This is a recipe for our signature guacamole dip. Our favorite way to serve it is with tortilla chips. It's so quick to make and needs just a few ingredients.

Makes: *1 bowl* | Time: *5 min*

Ingredients

- 3 ripe avocados, halved, pitted
- 1 teaspoon lemon juice
- ½ teaspoon of salt + more to taste
- ¼ cup (15 g) cilantro, chopped

Instructions

1. Cut vertical and horizontal lines into the avocados and remove their flesh with a spoon from the skin.

2. In a bowl, add the avocado chunks, lemon juice, salt, and cilantro and mash everything with a fork or potato masher. We like to leave ours a bit chunky, but you can make yours smooth by mashing it until really fine.

3. Enjoy with some vegan tortilla chips or veggie sticks.

Bianca's Kitchen Hack
How to Pick Ripe Avocados

The trick is to try to remove the stem. It should come off easily. If it is green beneath, it is a good sign the avocado is ripe. If it is brown underneath, the avocado is overripe and will have brown spots inside. If the stem does not come off, the avocado is not yet ripe.

HOMEMADE CRACKERS
(5 WAYS)

BASIC CRACKERS

Both of us are huge snack eaters, and homemade crackers are one of our favorite snack recipes to serve at parties or to munch on while bingeing TV shows. You'll find our basic recipe for crackers below, followed by a few fun variations and twists.

Makes: *2 cups* | Time: *35 min*

Instructions

1. Preheat the oven to 400°F/200°C.

2. In a mixing bowl, add in the dry ingredients, and whisk together. Then, add in the olive oil and water, and mix. Knead with your hand until it's a smooth dough. Add more flour if your dough is too sticky.

3. On a floured baking sheet lined with parchment paper, roll out the dough until as thin and even as possible. Use more flour if you need to.

4. Cut the dough with a pizza cutter into individual crackers.

5. Bake them in the oven for about 20 minutes until they become crispy and golden brown.

Ingredients

1 2/3 cups (200 g) all-purpose flour

½ teaspoon baking powder

½ teaspoon salt

1 teaspoon olive oil

½ cup (120 ml) water

SPINACH & SESAME CRACKERS

Additional Ingredients

- 1 tablespoon white sesame seeds
- 2 loosely packed cups (80 g) fresh spinach

Instructions

1. Wash the spinach and put it in a blender together with the water from the basic cracker recipe instructions (see on pg. 125) to give the crackers a green color, and blend until completely smooth. Follow the rest of the basic cracker recipe instructions with the following addition (see step below).

2. Add white sesame seeds to the dry ingredients before adding the wet ingredients.

CURRIED CRACKERS

Additional Ingredients

- 1 tablespoon black sesame seeds
- ½ teaspoon mild curry powder
- ½ teaspoon turmeric powder

Instructions

1. Follow the basic cracker recipe instructions (see on pg. 125) with the following addition (see step below).

2. Add the black sesame seeds, curry powder, and turmeric powder to the dry ingredients before adding the wet ingredients.

RED BEET CRACKERS

Instructions

1. Follow the basic cracker recipe instructions (see on pg. 125) with the following addition (see step below).

2. Substitute half (¼ cup) of the water with red beet juice for a lovely pink color before mixing the dough.

Additional Ingredients

¼ cup (60 ml) red beet juice

POPPY SEED CRACKERS

Instructions

1. Follow the basic cracker recipe instructions (see on pg. 125) with the following addition (see step below).

2. Add poppy seeds to the dry ingredients in step 2 and follow the base recipe.

Additional Ingredients

2 tablespoons poppy seeds

FATAL HUMMUS (4 WAYS)

1: Red Beet Hummus; 2: Cilantro Hummus;

3: Butternut Squash Hummus; 4: Basic Hummus

BASIC HUMMUS

Hummus, the beloved dip/spread made out of chickpeas, is a vegan staple. We want to show you a quick and easy way to make hummus yourself, including lots of options for variations, so you'll never get bored of it! Feel free to get creative where you can and try your own flavors and twists—hummus is very forgiving.

Makes: *1½ cups* | Time: *5 min*

Instructions

1. Put all the ingredients in your food processor or blender.

2. Blend or process until smooth (add more water if the consistency is too thick).

3. For variations, add the following additional ingredients in step 1.

Ingredients

- 1½ cups (250 g) canned chickpeas, drained and rinsed
- 1 tablespoon tahini
- ¾ teaspoon salt
- 1 teaspoon olive oil
- 1 tablespoon lemon juice
- 1 tablespoon water + more to thin out

CILANTRO HUMMUS

Instructions

1. Add stalks of cilantro to our basic hummus and process in a blender until smooth.

Ingredients

- 1½ cups Basic Hummus (see recipe above)
- 4 stalks cilantro

BUTTERNUT SQUASH HUMMUS

Ingredients

- 1½ cups basic hummus (see recipe on pg. 129)
- 1 cup (220 g) roasted butternut squash

Instructions

1. Add roasted butternut squash to our basic hummus and process in a blender until smooth.

RED BEET HUMMUS

Ingredients

- 1½ cups basic hummus (see recipe on pg. 129)
- 1½ tablespoons red beet juice

Instructions

1. Add red beet juice to our basic hummus and process in a blender until smooth.

BAKED HUMMUS DIP

Hummus is considered a vegan staple for various reasons, but have you tried it warm? In the form of a delicious baked hummus dip? For this version, we've mixed our basic hummus recipe with spinach, which makes it the perfect dip for parties!

Makes: *1½ cups* | Time: *50 min*

Instructions

1. Preheat the oven to 400°F/200°C.

2. Mix our basic hummus with the defrosted spinach and olive oil and transfer it to an oven-safe pan.

3. Bake the hummus dip for about 40 minutes.

4. Top with sliced scallions and halved cherry tomatoes and serve with tortilla chips, any of our homemade crackers (see on pg. 124) or veggie sticks.

Ingredients

- 1 cup (250 g) hummus (see on p. 130) or store-bought

- ½ cup (50 g) defrosted spinach

- 1 teaspoon olive oil

- A few thinly sliced scallions

- 3 cherry tomatoes, halved

CHEESY DILL POPCORN

Cheesy dill popcorn: the perfect snack for lazy days full of binge-watching TV. Thank you, nutritional yeast, for making everything taste like cheese. We love you.

Makes: *1 large bowl* | Time: *10 min*

Ingredients

- 1 tablespoon coconut oil
- ¼ cup (60 g) popcorn kernels
- ½ teaspoon salt
- 1½ tablespoons nutritional yeast
- ½ teaspoon dried dill

Instructions

1. In a large pot, heat the coconut oil on medium to high heat; toss in 3 popcorn kernels and close the lid (preferably a transparent one, so you can see what's going on inside).

2. Once the kernels have popped, take the pot off the burner and add in the rest of the kernels. Give the pot a quick shake and let it sit for 30 seconds before placing back on the burner. Then, place the pot back on the burner and let it cook on medium to high heat until all the kernels have popped.

3. Transfer the popcorn to a large bowl, sprinkle the salt, nutritional yeast, and dried dill on top, and give it a good shake. Done.

CHEESY PARTY POTATOES

The crispy potato rounds are loaded with our vegan cheese sauce, tomatoes, green olives, and lots of cilantro, which makes it the ideal party snack—or a special treat for when you're craving potatoes. You can easily double or triple the recipe depending on how many people you want to serve.

Makes: *1 large plate* | Time: *45 min*

Instructions

1. Preheat the oven to 480°F/250°C.

2. Use a mandoline slicer to thickly slice the potatoes.

3. Put potato slices in a large bowl and add the olive oil, salt, curry powder, paprika powder, and dried rosemary. Give it a good mix until the slices are coated.

4. Transfer the coated potato slices to a baking tray lined with parchment paper and spread them so they lay flat, not overlapping each other.

5. Bake them in the oven for about 20 to 30 minutes until golden and crisp on the edges.

6. Transfer them to a plate, drizzle with the cheese sauce, and top with tomato cubes, green olives, and chopped cilantro and dig in!

Ingredients

3 large potatoes

1 tablespoon olive oil

½ teaspoon salt

¼ teaspoon curry powder

¼ teaspoon paprika powder

½ teaspoon dried rosemary

3 tablespoons cheese sauce (see on pg. 18)

½ tomato, cubed

¼ cup (35 g) green olives, sliced

1 small bunch of cilantro, chopped

CRISPY SWEET 'N' SALTY CHICKPEAS

Oven roasted chickpeas are one of our favorite healthy snacks. Our recipe makes for a decent little batch of sweet and salty chickpeas that will make your binge-watching weekends even more of a thing to look forward to. Feel free to play around with different seasonings such as lemon, dill, curry powder, parsley, and garlic or sugar, cinnamon, and cocoa powder for sweet versions.

Makes: *1½ cups* | Time: *35 min*

Ingredients

- 17 oz. (480 g) canned chickpeas, drained, rinsed
- 1 teaspoon olive oil
- ½ teaspoon salt
- ½ teaspoon mild paprika powder
- Maple syrup, for drizzling

Instructions

1. Preheat the oven to 400°F/200°C.

2. Pat the chickpeas dry with a clean kitchen towel (don't worry about removing the skins unless they come off while drying).

3. Place the chickpeas on a baking sheet lined with parchment paper, and drizzle with olive oil, salt, and paprika powder. Give it a good mix so they're all coated.

4. Put them in the oven for about 30 to 45 minutes until they're crispy. Toss them around every 10 minutes to prevent them from burning.

5. When they're ready, drizzle the maple syrup over them and give them a good mix.

6. And enjoy! They are the crispiest while they're still hot, but I like them cooled down, too.

Sascha's Landmine Situation
When Traveling Abroad

Traveling abroad is tricky, especially when you're heading to a country where people don't really worry about veganism. If you like to travel to cities, you're in luck. Helpful websites like happycow.net or vegguide.org specialize in finding vegan options for you. These websites can help you get to know the city beforehand so that you can make it a foodie adventure. Consider buying and hoarding snacks. Stay at a hotel or apartment with a small kitchen (even a microwave can do wonders!). Look for Asian restaurants, as they often offer some kind of veggie sushi dish. Keep an eye out for Italian restaurants—if they're doing it properly, and some don't, then there should be no eggs or dairy in their pasta and pizza. But most importantly: Don't be afraid to ask. You will be surprised at how flexible restaurants can be.

GARLIC HERB BREADSTICKS

Fancy breadsticks are always a great snack for parties. You can serve them with different dips or eat them plain. Rolling the breadsticks can be quite exhausting, so we recommend having a helper when you plan on making breadsticks for a larger crowd!

Makes: *16 breadsticks* | Time: *30 min*

Instructions

1. Preheat the oven to 400°F/200°C.

2. In a small pot on low heat, add the coconut oil, parsley, oregano, minced garlic, and salt. Give it a good mix until the coconut oil is melted.

3. Cut the Multi-Purpose Bread dough into 16 equal parts and roll each one into ropes between your hands. Repeat for all the breadsticks.

4. Transfer the breadsticks onto a baking tray lined with parchment paper.

5. Brush the breadsticks with the herb garlic oil, then bake them in the oven for about 5 to 10 minutes, until golden.

Ingredients

2 tablespoons coconut oil

1 tablespoon chopped parsley

1 tablespoon chopped oregano

2 garlic cloves, minced

¼ teaspoon salt

1 portion Multi-Purpose Bread dough (see on pg. 110)

SWEET & SAVORY MANGO SALSA

This colorful, crowd-pleasing mango salsa is the ideal addition for any party, and just the last-minute recipe you were looking for. You can make this in 10 short minutes. Cut up all the fruits and veggies and give it a quick mix in a bowl. Serve it with tortilla chips and enjoy the happy faces of your guests!

Makes: *1 bowl* | Time: *10 min*

Ingredients

- 1 mango, peeled, pitted, diced
- 1 tomato, diced
- ¼ red bell pepper, diced
- ¼ small red onion, diced
- 1 small avocado, peeled, pitted, diced
- 1 tablespoon fresh cilantro, chopped
- 1 teaspoon fresh mint, chopped
- ¼ teaspoon salt
- 1 teaspoon lemon juice

Instructions

1. Add the diced mango and veggies in a bowl.
2. Add the herbs, salt, and lemon juice. Give it a quick mix.
3. Serve with tortilla chips.

Get-Togethers and Parties

This is an easy one. Bonding over food is a great way to learn about new people. However, it can be considered rude to decline all the food the host has been slaving away to make. Here's a simple, easy solution: Tell your host about your preferences beforehand and offer to bring something. Many party hosts spend the majority of their day preparing everything for the party to be a success, so in most cases they're happy to receive some help.

"TO SHARE OR NOT TO SHARE" PIZZA PINWHEELS

We are suckers for bite-sized party foods. We love hosting parties, having friends over, and offering them way too much food. No one goes home hungry on our watch! These vegan pizza pinwheels are our go-to treat because they can be made in only a couple of minutes, you can toy around with different fillings, and you can prepare them in advance. Instead of using Cashew Parmesan, you could also spread some of our vegan cheese sauce in there (see recipe on pg. 18), but don't use more than ⅓ of a cup or it will get too messy.

Makes: *30 pinwheels* | Time: *25 min*

Instructions

1. Preheat the oven to 400°F/200°C.

2. Roll out the puff pastry dough.

3. Spread the tomato passata on the puff pastry dough, but don't spread it on the bottom quarter or the tomato sauce will be squeezed out when rolling in the dough.

4. Sprinkle the garlic powder, salt, oregano, basil, and Cashew Parmesan on top.

5. Cut the olives in smaller pieces and sprinkle on top.

6. Roll up the puff pastry dough as tight as possible and close the edge.

7. Cut the puff pastry dough roll in about 30 pieces.

8. Place the pizza pinwheels on a baking tray lined with parchment paper (don't worry if they don't look perfect, they will puff up just the same!) and bake them in the oven for 15 to 20 minutes.

9. Enjoy them warm or let them cool off.

Ingredients

1 (9 x 16-inch) vegan puff pastry dough*

¼ cup (65 g) tomato passata

1 pinch of garlic powder

¼ teaspoon salt

½ teaspoon dried or fresh oregano

½ teaspoon dried or fresh basil

1 tablespoon Cashew Parmesan (see on pg. 17)

½ cup (65 g) green pitted olives

*If you can't find vegan puff pastry, you can also use store-bought or homemade pizza dough instead, but you will have to bake the pinwheels longer depending on the thickness of the dough.

SHAKE & BAKE SWEET POTATO FRIES

Whether you make these Sweet Potato Fries for a party or as a side dish, everyone loves them! With the shake & bake method you can coat them quickly and evenly in cornstarch and spices. They are delicious with our tzatziki dip (see on pg. 159).

Makes: *2 servings* | Time: *50 min*

Ingredients

- 3 medium-size sweet potatoes
- 2 teaspoons cornstarch
- 1 tablespoon olive oil
- ½ teaspoon salt
- ½ teaspoon cinnamon powder
- ½ teaspoon curry powder
- 1 dash of cayenne pepper
- Fresh parsley for garnish

Instructions

1. Preheat oven to 400°F/200°C.

2. Peel the sweet potatoes and cut them into even fries.

3. Put the sweet potato fries in a re-sealable bag (alternatively, you can do all of this in a large bowl) and add the cornstarch. Give it a good shake until they are all coated. Then, add the olive oil and spices to the bag and shake again until coated equally.

4. Transfer the fries to a baking sheet lined with parchment paper and spread them so they don't overlap each other.

5. Bake in the oven for about 15 minutes, then flip them and bake for another 10 to 15 minutes.

6. Let them cool off a bit before serving, and garnish with fresh parsley.

SLT SANDWICH

Seitan-lettuce-tomato (SLT) is the perfect alternative for the traditional bacon-lettuce-tomato sandwiches, best known as the BLT. We're using our homemade seitan for the recipe. And instead of mayo, we're using mashed avocados, which adds a nice creaminess. This is a great snack or take-to-work-lunch!

Makes: *2 sandwiches* | Time: *10 min*

Instructions

1. In a pan with olive oil, heat the seitan on medium to high heat for 3 to 4 minutes until crispy on both sides.

2. Add avocado slices on each of the bread slices and mash them a bit.

3. On one bread slice, add the lettuce, sliced tomatoes, crispy seitan. Top with another slice of bread. Enjoy!

Ingredients

½ teaspoon olive oil

4 slices seitan (see on pg. 21) or store-bought

4 slices bread (see our homemade Sunflower & Flaxseed Bread on pg. 117)

½ ripe avocado, peeled, pitted

4 lettuce leaves

1 tomato, sliced

SAUCES & DRESSINGS

DATE-SWEETENED BBQ SAUCE

This BBQ sauce is date-sweetened and the perfect condiment for cookouts. Use it to marinate or serve with grilled veggies, roasted tofu, or tempeh.

Makes: *1 cup* | Time: *30 min*

Ingredients

- 1 teaspoon olive oil
- 2 garlic cloves, minced
- 1 small red onion, chopped
- 4 soft dates, pitted, chopped
- 1 teaspoon paprika powder
- ½ teaspoon salt
- ⅓ cup (80 ml) red grape juice
- ½ cup (125 g) tomato passata
- ¼ teaspoon sriracha
- ¼ teaspoon liquid smoke

Instructions

1. In a pot on medium heat, add the olive oil, garlic, red onion, and dates and cook until the onions are translucent.

2. Add paprika powder and salt, give it a quick mix, and deglaze with red grape juice.

3. Then, add tomato passata, sriracha, and liquid smoke and let it simmer for about 5 to 10 minutes.

4. Let it cool off a bit before adding everything to a blender or use an immersion blender to blend until smooth.

5. Fill the BBQ sauce in a clean glass jar and store it in the fridge for about 1 week.

Sascha's Landmine Situation
BBQs

BBQs are all kinds of tricky. More often than not, the main topic is how to prepare the meat, cook the meat, and if the meat is ready. So, it seems that the odds are against you. First, it really all depends on how comfortable you feel in your group. If they know and accept your preferences and have finally gotten over joking about your vegan bratwurst, fine. However, prepare to be the butt of a number of lighthearted jokes about your food. Secondly, think beforehand about what principles you are willing to give up. If you don't care for your food touching theirs, it might be good to make the (hopefully understanding) grill master aware of your preferences beforehand. If that is not an option, you can always stick to the sides and salads. Bring enough to make you full, and then some—your friends will be curious, too.

CREAMY CILANTRO SAUCE

With just a few simple ingredients, you can make this delicious creamy green sauce that you can use as a dip or a salad dressing. Cilantrophobes can always sub the cilantro with fresh parsley and/or basil!

Makes: *½ cup* | Time: *5 min*

Instructions

1. Add all the ingredients in a high-speed blender and blend until completely smooth.

Ingredients

¾ cup (180 g) full-fat coconut milk

²/₃ cup (95 g) sunflower seeds*

1 tablespoon lemon juice

½ teaspoon salt + more to taste

½ cup (25 g) fresh cilantro

¼ cup (60 ml) water**

---

*If your blender is not very powerful, you can soak the sunflower seeds for 2 to 3 hours, and drain and rinse them to make it easier for your blender to process.
**We suggest you start with less water if you need a thick sauce and add in more after to gradually thin it out.

THE BEST TAHINI MAPLE DRESSING

This simple-to-make but delicious tahini maple dressing is perfect for salads or to use as a sauce for Middle Eastern inspired dishes such as falafel or chickpea salads. The tahini adds a slight bitterness, which gets balanced out by the maple syrup. What a dream team!

Makes: *⅓ cup* | Time: *5 min*

Ingredients

- 1½ tablespoons tahini
- ½ teaspoon water
- 1 tablespoon maple syrup
- 1 tablespoon lemon juice
- ¼ teaspoon salt or to taste

Instructions

1. In a bowl, add the tahini, water, maple syrup, and lemon juice. Combine with a small whisk until creamy. Add salt and whisk again until combined. Add more water to thin it out if it's too thick.

2. Add the dressing to an airtight jar to store it in the fridge for up to 1 week. If it becomes too thick in the fridge, feel free to thin it out with water.

VEGAN TZATZIKI

Tzatziki is a yogurt-based sauce, which originates in Greece. The grated cucumber and dill add a lovely lightness to the sauce. It's an amazingly delicious dipping sauce for our sweet potato fries (see on pg. 146) or Mediterranean dishes like our baked eggplant with raisin walnut rice (see on pg. 89).

Makes: *1½ cups | 5 min*

Instructions

1. Put the grated cucumber on a clean kitchen towel and press out excess water.

2. Then, add the grated cucumber to the yogurt, and add the minced garlic and dill. Give it a good mix and add salt to taste.

3. Drizzle with olive oil and garnish with cucumber slices.

4. You can serve it immediately, but it will taste even better if you give it 2 to 3 hours for the garlic and dill flavors to emerge.

Ingredients

½ cup (70 g) grated cucumber

1 cup (250 g) unsweetened soy yogurt

1 small garlic clove, minced

¼ teaspoon dill, chopped

Salt to taste

½ teaspoon olive oil

Cucumber slices for garnish

DESSERTS

LEMON-GLAZED CINNAMON ROLLS

For these cinnamon rolls, we are using a slightly adapted, sweet version of our Multi-Purpose Bread dough (see on pg. 110). These cinnamon rolls are topped with a delicious lemon glaze, which makes them the perfect Sunday treat.

Makes: *12 rolls* | Time: *1½ hours + 2 hours rising time*

Instructions

1. For the yeast dough, add the flour and white sugar in a large mixing bowl, and combine. Make a well in the middle, and add in the dry yeast and ¼ cup of the milk. Let it rest for about 10 minutes. You can be sure it's working if the yeast gets bubbly.

2. Add in the salt, 1 tablespoon of coconut oil, and the remaining rice milk. Combine with a large spoon. Then, use your hands to form a soft dough.

3. Let the dough sit covered under a clean kitchen towel in a warm spot for 1½ to 2 hours until it doubles in size.

4. Preheat the oven to 400°F/200°C.

5. Transfer the dough to a baking tray covered with floured parchment paper and roll it out to a rectangle.

6. For the cinnamon sugar sprinkling, combine ¼ cup of white sugar and cinnamon.

7. Brush the dough with about ⅔ of the remaining liquid coconut oil and sprinkle the cinnamon and sugar mixture on top.

8. Carefully roll the dough in and cut it into 12 slices.

9. Lightly coat a 7 x 10-inch baking pan with oil, put in the cinnamon rolls, and brush the tops with the rest of the liquid coconut oil. Bake them in the oven for about 20 to 30 minutes until golden on top.

10. For the lemon glaze, put the ingredients in a small bowl and whisk until well combined. Drizzle the lemon glaze on top of the cinnamon rolls before serving.

Ingredients for the Yeast Dough

4 cups (480 g) all-purpose flour

2 tablespoons vegan white sugar

2 teaspoons active dry yeast

1¼ cups (300 ml) lukewarm rice milk

1 pinch of salt

2 tablespoons liquid coconut oil, divided

Ingredients for the Cinnamon Sugar Sprinkling

¼ cup (50 g) vegan white sugar

1 teaspoon cinnamon

Ingredients for the Lemon Glaze

½ cup (65 g) powdered sugar

1 tablespoon rice milk

1 teaspoon lemon zest

Visiting Relatives

Oftentimes, visiting relatives is all about food, the lunches, dinners, birthday cakes, among others. Grandmas are the best cooks, because they use a lot of fat, and fatty foods are delicious. Most vegans eventually learn that grandmas use butter for everything. Chances are that she will try to veganize your favorite birthday cake only to casually mention the single egg she used to make it work.

There are solutions to this: Older relatives often tend to take a lot of pride in doing everything by themselves, but you can insist on bringing some food yourself. Another solution would be to offer to help in the kitchen. The best way to make veganism less weird is to show people that it's really not. We've heard more than one story of grandmas saying something among the lines of "this is how our mother used to do it when we were children." Many people don't realize that vegan food wasn't that uncommon in generations past, it's just that nobody called it that.

APPLE PIE MUFFINS

Homemade apple pie can be quite a piece of work. However, these amazing apple pie muffins can be made quickly and easily. As a plus, this fistful of baked heaven will give you that warm, delicious taste of an apple pie.

Makes: *9 muffins* | Time: *30 min*

Instructions

1. Preheat oven to 360°F/180°C.

2. In a mixing bowl, combine all the dry ingredients except the apple and powdered sugar for the muffins, whisk, then add all the wet ingredients and whisk again until it's a smooth batter. Add in ¾ of the apple cubes.

3. Add the batter to muffin wrappers or a lightly oiled muffin pan, and sprinkle the rest of the apple cubes on top of each muffin. Put the tray in the oven for about 15 to 20 minutes. See Bianca's Kitchen Hack below to make sure the muffins are baked all the way through.

4. Dust with powdered sugar before serving!

Bianca's Kitchen Hack
How to Test Baked Goods for Doneness

The easiest way to test your muffins, cakes, and other baked goods if they are baked all the way through is by sticking a thin wooden stick or toothpick in. If it comes out pretty much clean, maybe with a few crumbs here or there, it's done. If the stick comes out wet with batter on it, it's not done yet.

Ingredients

- 1¼ cups (150 g) all-purpose flour
- ¼ cup (50 g) vegan white sugar
- 1 teaspoon baking powder
- ¼ teaspoon baking soda
- 1 teaspoon cinnamon powder
- 1 pinch of salt
- 1 tablespoon neutral vegetable oil e.g. coconut oil
- 2/3 cup (160 ml) unsweetened plant-based milk e.g. rice milk
- ½ teaspoon apple cider vinegar
- ½ teaspoon vanilla extract
- 1 sweet apple, peeled, core removed, cubed
- Powdered sugar for dusting the top

CHOCOLATE-COVERED ALMOND CAKE

This is a simple recipe for a chocolate-covered almond cake. This no-nonsense cake can be devoured as is or used as a base. Also, you can simply whisk the ingredients for the cake in one bowl, which means minimal cleanup!

Makes: *1 cake* | Time: *40 min*

Ingredients for Almond Cake

- 1⅓ cups (160 g) all-purpose flour
- ⅓ cup + 1 tablespoon (80 g) vegan white sugar
- ½ cup (50 g) almond meal
- 1½ teaspoons baking powder
- ½ teaspoon baking soda
- 1 teaspoon coconut oil, liquid
- ½ teaspoon apple cider vinegar
- 1 cup (240 ml) plant-based milk such as rice milk

Ingredients for Chocolate Coating

- ¾ cup (100 g) baking chocolate or chocolate chips
- 1 teaspoon coconut oil

Instructions

1. Preheat the oven to 360°F/180°C.

2. Place all the dry ingredients for the almond cake in a mixing bowl and combine. Add in the wet ingredients and whisk until a smooth batter is formed.

3. Lightly oil an 8 x 8-inch baking pan and pour in the cake batter. Bake in the oven for 25 minutes. Test with a toothpick (see Bianca's Kitchen Hack on pg. 165) to make sure the cake is baked all the way through.

4. Let the cake cool down for 2 to 3 hours.

5. For the chocolate coating, heat the chocolate together with the coconut oil in a double boiler or microwave, and combine. Pour the melted chocolate over the cooled cake and spread it around the cake so it's covered evenly. Place it in the fridge for about 5 to 10 minutes until the chocolate has set.

CARAMEL CUPS

These vegan caramel cups are everything you've ever wanted—you haven't realized it yet. With roasted peanuts and our super simple ooey-gooey caramel sauce covered in chocolate, the addiction potential for these is alarmingly high.

Makes: *6 cups* | Time: *30 min*

Instructions

1. Place 6 muffin liners in a muffin pan or use silicone muffin liners.

2. In a double boiler or microwave, melt the baking chocolate/chocolate chips and coconut oil, and stir well.

3. Use about half the chocolate for this step. Fill about 1½ teaspoons of melted chocolate in each cup, and tilt the muffin pan or silicone liners so the chocolate spreads to all sides. Place the muffin pan in the fridge for a few minutes (until the chocolate hardens).

4. Roast the peanuts with a pinch of salt in a small pan on medium heat for about 3 to 4 minutes while stirring occasionally. Chop the peanuts into smaller pieces.

5. Once the first chocolate layer has set, divide the caramel sauce into the muffin liners (place it in the middle), and sprinkle the peanuts on top.

6. Top the cups with the rest of the melted chocolate. Tilt the pan/liners a bit so the tops of the cups are completely covered with the chocolate. Let the cups harden in the fridge for about 5 minutes.

7. Once the chocolate is hardened, carefully remove the cups from the cupcake liners and enjoy!

8. Store the Caramel cups in the fridge until they are all gone (which shouldn't take that long).

Ingredients

- 1¼ cups (190 g) vegan baking chocolate or chocolate chips
- 1 teaspoon coconut oil
- ¼ cup (40 g) raw or roasted peanuts*
- 1 pinch of salt
- 1 portion caramel sauce (see on pg. 25)

*If using already roasted peanuts, skip step 3.

EAT-IN-ONE-SITTING APPLE STRUDEL

Apple strudel is a typical Austrian dessert made with puff pastry, apples, and cinnamon. As a kid, Bianca used to eat a whole strudel by herself; now she has to share with Sascha. So sad. Add raisins or sliced nuts for variations.

Makes: *1 strudel* | Time: *20 min*

Ingredients

- 1 package 9 x 16-inch vegan puff pastry dough
- 2 apples, the sweet kind e.g. Pink Lady, peeled, core and seeds removed
- 1 teaspoon cinnamon
- Powdered sugar for dusting the top

Instructions

1. Preheat oven to 350°F/180°C and take the vegan pastry dough out of the fridge to thaw.

2. Slice the apples with a mandoline slicer or cut by hand into very thin slices.

3. Put sliced apple into a bowl and add in the cinnamon. Mix well, and don't worry about broken apple slices.

4. Put the thawed dough on a baking sheet lined with parchment paper. Put the apple-cinnamon mixture on the top half of the pastry dough and fold it in. Press the edges together.

5. Bake the apple strudel in the oven for about 15 to 20 minutes, until golden brown.

6. Dust the strudel with powdered sugar before serving. You can eat it warm or cold—it's delicious either way.

BERRY SWIRL POPS

These berry swirl yogurt pops are the perfect refreshment for those long, hot summer days. Not only are these pops super easy to make with only three ingredients, but they also look super pretty with the swirled mixed berries!

Makes: *8 pops* | Time: *10 min + at least 4 hours freezing time*

Instructions

1. Heat the frozen berry mix together with the maple syrup in a small pot on low to medium heat for a couple of minutes until it thickens.

2. Then, spoon a drop of soy yogurt into each of the 8 ice pop molds, followed by the berry mixture (use about half of it in this step), then add a drop of yogurt again, followed by the rest of the berry mixture. Use a skewer to give the mixture a light swirl. Then, top each ice pop mold with another drop of soy yogurt.

3. Insert the stick and freeze for at least 4 hours or overnight.

Ingredients

1 cup (130 g) frozen berry mix

1 teaspoon maple syrup

2 cups (500 g) plant-based yogurt e.g. soy yogurt*

*If you're using unsweetened soy yogurt, stir in another teaspoon of maple syrup to sweeten it.

BLENDER BROWNIES WITH CHOCOLATE AVOCADO FROSTING

You've read that right—the batter for these brownies can be made in a blender! Not only does this mean minimal cleanup, but it's also quick and easy to make. We've topped these brownies with a decadent avocado frosting and cocoa nibs. They taste so rich, you would never guess they are vegan!

Makes: *6 servings* | Time: *50 min + 3 hours cooling time*

Ingredients for Brownies

- 1 cup (140 g) oat flour
- ½ cup (60 g) almond meal
- 7 soft dates, pitted
- 1 pinch of salt
- 3 ripe bananas, peeled
- ¼ cup (25 g) cocoa powder
- 1 tablespoon plant-based milk e.g. rice milk

Ingredients for Chocolate Avocado Frosting

- 3 avocados, peeled, pitted
- 1 ripe banana, peeled
- 2 tablespoons plant-based milk e.g. rice milk
- 2 tablespoons cocoa powder
- 2 tablespoons maple syrup

Additional Ingredient

- 1 tablespoon cocoa nibs

Instructions

1. Preheat oven to 320°F/160°C and line a 7 x 10-inch loaf pan with parchment paper.

2. Add the oat flour and almond meal to your blender. Pulse until fine. Then, add the dates, salt, bananas, cocoa powder, and plant-based milk and blend until smooth and creamy. You might have to scrape down the sides a couple of times.

3. Transfer the batter to the baking pan and flatten the surface.

4. Bake for about 25 minutes and let it cool off completely for 2 to 3 hours.

5. For the chocolate avocado frosting, add all the ingredients to a blender and blend until completely smooth. You might also have to scrape down the sides a few times.

6. Once the brownies are completely cool, pour the chocolate avocado chocolate frosting on top and add the cocoa nibs. Cut into brownies. You can eat the them immediately, but it's better if you let them sit in the fridge for about 3 hours to let the frosting thicken a bit.

7. The brownies can be stored in the fridge for 3 to 4 days.

OUR FAVORITE CHOCOLATE CHIP COOKIES

These easy chocolate chip cookies are crisp on the outside, but soft and flakey on the inside. They are made with simple ingredients, which you probably have at home already. Don't worry, you won't need any kind of egg substitute. You know what goes really well with these? Our homemade almond milk (see on pg. 22).

Makes: *4 large cookies* | Time: *20 min*

Instructions

1. Preheat the oven to 350°F/180°C.

2. Add the coconut oil and white sugar in a mixing bowl and mix with an electric hand mixer until combined. Add the flour, baking powder, and salt, and mix again until mixture is crumbly. Then, add in the plant-based milk and mix until combined. Add in 1 tablespoon of chocolate chips and give another quick mix until the chips are all incorporated into the cookie batter.

3. Using an ice cream scoop, put four balls of cookie dough onto a baking tray lined with parchment paper. Press them flat a bit, and add the a few more chocolate chips on top of each cookie.

4. Bake the cookies for about 10 to 15 minutes, until the edges are golden. It's going to be a tough wait, but it's best to let them cool down a bit before eating.

Ingredients

- 2 tablespoons coconut oil, solid
- 2 tablespoons vegan white sugar
- 2/3 cup (80 g) all-purpose flour
- 1/8 teaspoon baking powder
- 1 pinch of salt
- 4 teaspoons plant-based milk e.g. rice milk
- 1 tablespoon chocolate chips + a few more to add on top

FANCY APPLE ROSES

These fancy-looking apple roses are the perfect dessert to impress your family and friends. They are way easier to make than they look: You'll only need puff pastry, cinnamon, sugar, and an apple. Bake them in a muffin pan, so that they keep their shape.

Makes: *6 apple roses* | Time: *45 min*

Ingredients

- 1 sweet apple e.g. Pink Lady
- 1 (9 x 16-inch) package vegan puff pastry, thawed
- 1 teaspoon vegan white sugar
- ½ teaspoon cinnamon
- powdered sugar for dusting

Instructions

1. Preheat oven to 350°F/180°C.
2. Slice the apple with a mandoline slicer into very thin slices.
3. Roll out the puff pastry and sprinkle the white sugar and cinnamon evenly on the pastry dough.
4. Cut the dough horizontally into 6 equal strips.
5. Place the apple slices on the pastry dough strips so that they overlap one another. The skin side of the apples should stick a little out of the strip. Carefully roll the strips in.
6. Smooth down the bottom and press it together a bit.
7. Place the apple roses in a lightly oiled muffin pan and put the pan in the oven on the lowest rack for about 25 to 30 minutes.
8. Let them cool off completely before carefully twisting them out of the pan.
9. Dust the apple roses with powdered sugar before serving.

LIFE-CHANGING FROZEN CHOCOLATE

Did you know that you can make your own, healthier version of chocolate? You just need three ingredients, which you probably have at home already, for this frozen chocolate. This is a very basic chocolate recipe, so feel free to add nuts, raisins, cocoa nibs, or whatever you prefer.

Makes: *10 chocolate pieces* | Time: *5 min*

Instructions

1. Heat the coconut oil in a small pot until liquefied. Then, take the pot off the stove and add in the maple syrup. Whisk it together.

2. Add in the cocoa powder and whisk again until everything comes together and the mixture is nice and smooth.

3. Fill the chocolate in molds and put in the freezer for at least 6 hours or overnight. Make sure to store them in the freezer—they melt pretty quickly!

Ingredients

- 2 tablespoons coconut oil
- 2 tablespoons maple syrup
- 3 tablespoons cocoa powder

ONE-INGREDIENT NICE CREAM

4 WAYS

1: Basic; 2: Peanut Butter;
3: Strawberry; 4: Chocolate

BASIC NICE CREAM

You can make the best, healthiest, and most minimalistic ice cream with only one base ingredient: bananas. And while we love the most basic version with bananas only, we'd like to show you three different variations that we love!

Makes: *1 serving* | Time: *5 min*

Instructions

1. Peel the banana, break it in chunks, and put it in a zip lock or freezer-friendly container. Freeze overnight.

2. Place the frozen banana chunks in a food processor and pulse until a creamy banana ice cream is formed. Don't give up on the ice cream too soon; it might look like it's not working, but if you give it a bit of time, you'll eventually get there! You might have to scrape down the sides a few times. That's it!

3. Garnish with our caramel sauce (see on pg. 25), chopped, roasted peanuts, cocoa nibs, or freeze-dried strawberries.

Ingredients

2 ripe bananas

PEANUT BUTTER NICE CREAM

Ingredients

- 2 bananas, peeled, frozen, cut in chunks
- 2 tablespoons peanut butter

Instructions

1. Add frozen banana chunks and peanut butter to a food processor and pulse until creamy.

STRAWBERRY NICE CREAM

Ingredients

- 1 banana, peeled, frozen, cut in chunks
- ½ cup (65 g) strawberries, frozen

Instructions

1. Add frozen banana chunks and frozen strawberries to a food processor and pulse until creamy.

CHOCOLATE NICE CREAM

Ingredients

- 2 bananas, peeled, frozen, cut in chunks
- 2 tablespoons cocoa powder
- 2 teaspoons plant-based milk e.g. homemade almond milk (see on pg. 22)

Instructions

1. Add frozen banana chunks, cocoa powder, and plant-based milk to a food processor and pulse until creamy.

NO-BAKE LIME BLUEBERRY CHEESECAKE

This frozen, no-bake lime blueberry cheesecake is the perfect goodie for hot summer days. Instead of blueberries, you can use any fruit your heart desires, or use a swirl of our caramel sauce (see on pg. 25).

Makes: *4 mini cheesecakes* | Time: *15 min + 5 hours waiting time*

Instructions

1. For the crust, place the blanched almonds in a food processor and process for about 40 seconds. Add the maple syrup and coconut oil and process again until the mixture sticks together when you press it together with your fingers.

2. For the filling, place all the ingredients except the blueberries in a high-speed blender and blend until completely smooth.

3. Lightly oil four 6-ounce freezer-friendly ramekins and line each with two parchment paper strips. This will help remove the cheesecake from the containers later.

4. Divide the crust mixture into the containers and press it flat with a spoon or your fingers. Add the cheesecake filling, top with blueberries, and put in the freezer for about 5 hours. Then, remove the cheesecake from the ramekins. We recommend giving them a quick thaw before eating.

Ingredients for the Crust

- ½ cup (75 g) blanched almonds
- 1 tablespoon maple syrup
- ½ tablespoon coconut oil, liquid

Ingredients for the Filling

- ½ cup (300 g) silken tofu
- ½ tablespoon lime zest
- 1 tablespoon lime juice
- 1 tablespoon coconut oil
- ¼ cup (50 g) vegan white sugar
- ¼ teaspoon vanilla extract
- 1 tablespoon plant-based milk e.g. almond milk
- 1 cup (100 g) fresh blueberries

THANKS

🐘 First and foremost, we want to thank the blog readers of ElephantasticVegan.com. If it weren't for you, a cookbook would have never been possible.

🐘 Thank you, Nicole Mele and the whole Skyhorse publishing team for believing in us, even though we are on the other side of the world.

🐘 Big thanks go to all of our friends and family, who bravely tried what we came up with in the kitchen.

🐘 We also want to thank all vegans and future vegans. The vegan movement wouldn't be there without you.

🐘 Thank you, dear reader, for buying the book, or maybe somebody gifted it to you, then thanks to them for buying—I guess we're stuck with each other now. We really hope you enjoy reading *The Beginner's Guide to Everyday Vegan Cooking* as much as we enjoyed writing it!

INDEX

CONVERSION CHARTS

METRIC AND IMPERIAL CONVERSIONS
(These conversions are rounded for convenience)

Ingredient	Cups/Tablespoons/Teaspoons	Ounces	Grams/Milliliters
Butter	1 cup = 16 tablespoons = 2 sticks	8 ounces	230 grams
Cheese, shredded	1 cup	4 ounces	110 grams
Cream cheese	1 tablespoon	0.5 ounce	14.5 grams
Cornstarch	1 tablespoon	0.3 ounce	8 grams
Flour, all-purpose	1 cup/1 tablespoon	4.5 ounces/0.3 ounce	125 grams/8 grams
Flour, whole wheat	1 cup	4 ounces	120 grams
Fruit, dried	1 cup	4 ounces	120 grams
Fruits or veggies, chopped	1 cup	5 to 7 ounces	145 to 200 grams
Fruits or veggies, puréed	1 cup	8.5 ounces	245 grams
Honey, maple syrup, or corn syrup	1 tablespoon	.75 ounce	20 grams
Liquids: cream, milk, water, or juice	1 cup	8 fluid ounces	240 milliliters
Oats	1 cup	5.5 ounces	150 grams
Salt	1 teaspoon	0.2 ounce	6 grams
Spices: cinnamon, cloves, ginger, or nutmeg (ground)	1 teaspoon	0.2 ounce	5 milliliters
Sugar, brown, firmly packed	1 cup	7 ounces	200 grams
Sugar, white	1 cup/1 tablespoon	7 ounces/0.5 ounce	200 grams/12.5 grams
Vanilla extract	1 teaspoon	0.2 ounce	4 grams

OVEN TEMPERATURES

Fahrenheit	Celsius	Gas Mark
225°	110°	¼
250°	120°	½
275°	140°	1
300°	150°	2
325°	160°	3
350°	180°	4
375°	190°	5
400°	200°	6
425°	220°	7
450°	230°	8